BEGINNER'S GUIDE
TO
SWIMMING AND WATER SAFETY

Beginner's Guide to Swimming and Water Safety

HARCOURT ROY

Illustrations by
Peter Ford
and
Roy L. Alexander

DRAKE PUBLISHERS INC
NEW YORK

ISBN 0-87749-411-8

DRAKE PUBLISHERS INC
381 *Park Avenue South*
New York, N.Y. 10016

© Harcourt Roy 1972

Printed in Great Britain

To my wife Janet

because her ideas and practice of teaching beginners
to swim are functionally direct and delightfully practical. She's been at it successfully for a good many
years and has a way with her. She certainly knows
what she's talking about—a fact the children recognise
and respond to readily and happily. A blessing!

Contents

7

Illustrations

9

Acknowledgements

We are concerned primarily with learning to swim for fun, fitness, health and personal safety. The total submersion and exercise of the near-naked body in clean, attractive water of an agreeable temperature is one of our most pleasurable, sensual delights—and our birthright. We love it in one form or another.

So we can especially appreciate the efforts of these twenty-one organisations of three western countries, for promoting these aims through their swimming and water-safety instruction over the years. I'm truly glad of this opportunity to introduce and thank them and the many others who contribute to the vital work of the National Water Safety Committee in Britain.

Great Britain:
Royal Life Saving Society (R.L.S.S.)
Royal Society for the Prevention of Accidents (RoSPA)
Amateur Swimming Association (A.S.A.)
Central Council of Physical Recreation (C.C.P.R.)
Scottish Council of Physical Recreation (S.C.P.R.)
English Schools Swimming Association (E.S.S.A.)
Swimming Teachers Association (S.T.A.)
Welsh Amateur Swimming Association (W.A.S.A.)
Scottish Amateur Swimming Association (S.A.S.A.)
Irish Amateur Swimming Association (I.A.S.A.)
Scout Association
Girl Guides Association

Canada:
Canadian Red Cross Society, Water Safety Service
National Council YMCA's of Canada
Boys Clubs of Canada
Boy Scouts of Canada
Girl Guides of Canada Inc.

America:
American Red Cross Society, Water Safety Service
Boys Clubs of America
Boy Scouts of America
Girl Scouts of America

My appreciation is likewise expressed for the special work with young children of Mrs. Virginia Hunt Newman of California, *Teaching an Infant to Swim*, 1967 (Angus & Robertson (U.K.) Ltd., 1968). She has a particular talent for developing water confidence and fundamental swimming ability with babies.

The remarkably successful beginners' swimming project at Craven Park Primary School in London, N.16, was started in the 1960s by Mr. H. V. Howard, Headmaster, and Mr. D. P. Grainger, Deputy Head at that time. Their marked success was the result of enthusiastic, realistic teaching using one of the first classroom, shallow-water learner pools of the same overall depth in London, maybe in Britain, along with a comfortable, enjoyable water temperature of 90° F. *Get Swimming: A Sure Guide to Confidence in the Water* is their book published by Souvenir Press Ltd., 1966.

The English Schools Swimming Association with their 'Swimming Bath Scheme' are doing very good work along these lines.

Then there was Fred Lanoue, Professor of Physical Education and Head Swimming Coach at the Georgia Institute of Technology in America, who did so much good work with his progressive *Drownproofing* technique, published by Prentice-Hall Inc., 1963.

He had plenty of critics (sceptics?), but nevertheless, his drownproofing method works with surprising effectiveness. Its functional simplicity and economy of effort appeals to me. In any case, I've never wanted to down-grade his system, because for me it has worked so well, so I'm happy to include a run-down of it here, my style.

When I was first a beginner by the sea, waters were not so polluted and unpleasant. It didn't enter one's head to worry about oil, sewage, plastics and chemical seepage poisoning the environment, as they do now, tragically.

Acknowledgements

Fortunately, some sections of our national and local authorities (unhappily, not yet all) are beginning to express an encouraging concern for the cleanliness and safety of our waters. I'm sure most of us hope they will develop a really firm, co-ordinated anti-pollution policy and apply it ruthlessly, for the benefit of everyone, before it's too late.

Some of our industrialists too, amazingly enough, are revealing an emerging conscience for the future habitability of our environment—which is also theirs! They do want this, don't they? We're lost if they don't.

If we all stick together, as we know we should, and develop this anti-pollution and conservation conscience, we stand a good chance of retaining, even increasing, safe, clean environmental water in which to enjoy our swimming and water-safety skills. We must have this above all for the health and happiness of our children to follow—tomorrow's world.

This is strengthened by the construction of public swimming pool complexes and the maintenance of clean, attractive and safe seaside swimming beaches around the country. We desperately want to see this movement develop unchecked. It will if we show that it is important to society. Can we?

Now let me give a big thank-you to *Health For All* magazine for allowing me to reproduce those 'Drownproofing' illustrations from an article I did for them in April 1968; and to Purley, Clark, Mermaid and Cranleigh Pools; Ware Safety Appliances; and Portex Limited, all for supplying necessary material and information. I do appreciate their co-operation and help.

Finally, if my two artistic friends, Peter Ford and Roy Alexander hadn't come so willingly to my aid at such short notice and produced the bulk of the art work, I don't suppose we should have got the book out this year. My sincere thanks here and now, boys.

HARCOURT ROY

Introduction

(P.F.)

FIG. 1. *Are you drownproof?*

THE SIMPLE APPROACH

The case for water-safety and survival of the non-swimmer, child or adult, is presented through a practical combination of water-confidence, basic drownproofing and elementary floating, rudimentary 'natural' swimming and fun-play, and simple water-entry from just above surface level. A 'Beginner's Swimming and Water-safety Test' is presented for this.

Orthodox and competitive swimming and diving is not included. This is not the place for it. That is the function of the school, youth organisation or private swimming club. A confidently drownproofed person will subsequently decide, with professional advice, how involved he or she will want to become in speed swimming and water-sports. This is no problem once the initial water-confidence and waterproofing have been mastered by the young child.

If a person has reached youth or adulthood without being able to swim or survive by their own efforts in deep water, the learning and survival processes described here can apply equally as well. It is never too late to become a swimmer, no matter how long you have left it before learning. This is the aspect we are primarily concerned about: helping non-swimmers to swim.

ABILITY TO 'DO NOTHING'

The most difficult water-skill for a non-swimmer to learn is the ability to '*do nothing*', because ingrained, misconceived psychological attitudes may have to be overcome. This means reconditioning the person's instinctive reaction upon entering deep water accidentally.

Understandably, they desperately strive to keep their head above water by kicking, thrashing and straining in a panic-stricken frenzy, dissipating valuable energy and generating greater panic. This 'mindless' activity will generally guarantee an early drowning, unless they are pulled from the water quickly by a calm and confident rescuer.

The antidote to this form of demise is to learn two basic water-skills *first*. (1) The ability to submerge completely, calmly and voluntarily and to feel genuinely at ease *under the surface by choice*. (2) The ability to float at the surface, completely relaxed, without tension or fear for an indefinite period of time.

Basically, we need to abolish the sinker's faulty, fear-stressed notion that he must do something vigorous with his arms and legs to survive.

Once these two skills are mastered, then learning to do *something* recognisable as swimming, is comparatively easy. This need only be a gentle finning movement with the hands and a non-vigorous flutter-kick while on the back; or the elementary 'Dog-Paddle' on the front.

WATER CONFIDENCE HAS PRIORITY

The acquirement of *water-confidence* is the first and foremost priority in any beginner's swimming programme. At first this is not synonymous with the person's ability to swim. Eventually it will be.

A person has water-confidence when he can be fully submerged from any form of entry, deliberate or accidental, and retain full command of his senses, control of his actions and have the ability to open his eyes and discover in which direction is the surface. Then take the right action to guarantee surfacing without tension or fear, before oxygen-starvation causes panic and involuntary opening of the mouth underwater.

The golden rule for underwater survival and subsequent surfacing is: EYES OPEN, MOUTH CLOSED, BRAIN ALERT, BODY RELAXED.

WHAT TO EXPECT

I won't 'go off the deep end' about cold climates, unsuitable facilities and the literally shocking temperature of most pools. But if the water is warm enough (a vital factor) you can float, loaf, glide, scull or paddle along lazily, or happily do nothing at all and feel how idyllic it is to be so utterly up-lifted, wrapped-around and effortlessly supported, exalting in such a friendly liquid environment.

Cooler water requires a different attitude, more determination no doubt, but this need not diminish the pleasure one little bit, once you are a swimmer. You'll simply react differently and dynamically. You can splash, frolic, jump, dive, swim and generally play about actively to keep your body temperature comfortable and your whole self stimulated. You'll do this all right, with lots of elation.

How you choose to enjoy yourself in pool, pond, lake, river or sea will always be decided by your level of skill and your confidence to do the right thing in any emergency—although with pre-knowledge and applied water-sense, accidents shouldn't occur. You'll have this.

You should be waterproofed, drownproofed, as much at ease and as safe in or under water as out of it. There certainly shouldn't be any conscious alienation or tension. You will be in your natural element. Well, let's say you can be—if you work at it and have the right help.

YOUR NATURAL ELEMENT?

If this all seems a bit too exaggerated to accept at face value, remember that water should be at least your second natural element, once you are born and exposed to the air. Before birth you were totally immersed in a membrane of fluid (the 'waters'), and babies are said to have a natural swimming reflex that works for them before they can walk (if the adult doesn't do anything to destroy it!).

Once you have learnt to float completely relaxed, can submerge free from tension like an otter, slide, glide, swim and play effortlessly to your heart's content in water of varying depth, you will feel released with both a conscious and an instinctive ease.

You will enjoy a relaxed naturalness in water. But some of it may be much deeper than your height, so you will have to acquire a complete independence of the bottom. And you can, even as an infant—or even as a middle-aged, non-physical type who may be resigned by now to imagining that he will never be able to swim. A misconception if there ever was one.

THE WATER IS THERE

Such a quality of performance and enjoyment, security and ease of existence in water, should be the birthright of everyone from baby to grandma: inland, because of rivers, lakes, canals, reservoirs, gravel pits, streams, ponds and pools; and for coastal dwellers, it goes without saying. You can't afford to be a non-swimmer wherever or whoever you are.

I'd like to help you fulfil this purpose. Mainly by encouraging your self-learning, and individual tuition rather than by class instruction, along with a partner whom you can trust. I don't recommend you to attempt your water education on your own. You wouldn't want to do anything foolish. But getting thoroughly acclimatised to water with a partner or buddy is an essential part of our commonsense survival system.

On the other hand, every adult too, from parent to school-teacher or club leader, who has someone needing to be taught how to swim; or who personally still needs to improve their own water-confidence can extract what they need for their own use, according to their own style, their choice.

The water is there, in great abundance, awaiting our pleasure. By all means, literally, let us enjoy it, whole-heartedly. It's certainly a shame to waste it.

PART ONE

Learner Pools and Equipment

It is a good idea to bring in an outline of these practical teaching pools at the beginning, so we can have a clear picture to start with of the type of pool most suited to our learning, or teaching needs. Having this clear understanding of just what is involved, will help us to look for and select the best type of pool (or body of water) for our special requirements. Whether we get it or not is still uncertain, no doubt; but at least we shall have the satisfaction of knowing what we ought to have. And achievement in the field is by no means impossible. It depends largely upon our incentive and determination.

CHAPTER ONE

Starting with Shallow Water and Depth Reduction

I am not writing advertising copy, so don't worry on that score. We have to buy our pools from some commercial specialist or other. There are several expert manufacturers in the 'field'. So we study and compare the leading firms' literature and specifications; then when we think we know just what we want —seek professional advice.

By commenting on the special requirements for learners and beginners at the start, I'm hoping to help you over the first hurdle. I'll mention one or two of the leading firms in Britain as we go along.

By the way, these first five sections are offered as an introduction, not as instruction. We get on to firm, direct teaching with Chapter 6. As for equipment, this is restricted to reaching and buoyancy aids. Actual pool filtration, purification and heating equipment is not given space in these pages. It would be an unnecessary repetition when the manufacturers provide far greater detail in their technical brochures and leaflets.

SHALLOW WATER

This is our greatest need for hazardous sinkers and nervous beginners; particularly where large classes are concerned, if we are teachers. We have a great responsibility here. At the same time, I accept that every reader isn't a teacher (nor is every parent, if you get my point!). Many may simply want to water-proof themselves and get swimming with the least possible trouble and anguish. That's what this book is for.

I don't know why puppies can swim first time and babies can't. Do you? Maybe we adults are too nervous or uncertain to try. We'll examine this later. But I am certain that if you do nothing to introduce fear of water, but everything to encourage confidence and self-awareness of natural floating ability in your infant—yes, infant, he will paddle around in water as readily as a puppy.

But you must start with shallow water. Forgive me if this is obvious. I'm sorry to say it doesn't seem obvious with all city and county authorities. So they create a most difficult and frustrating handicap by constructing the wrong type of pool to start with! A great pity, isn't it?

Another thing: it will require determination, effort and perseverance—from the adult. Perhaps this explains why so *few* pre-schoolers learn to swim. Not necessarily their fault!

FOR CRAWLERS AND INFANTS

A little further on we will be discussing 'Waterproofing Baby', which requires a different, personal technique and special patience. But don't let that throw you. Meanwhile, think in terms of a really shallow water pool. Just enough depth of water to let your older infant crawl about like a 'crocodile', breathing, of course. Having great fun too.

You (or rather he) will need from 8 to 12 inches plus of water. You may protest: 'Where am I going to find that, except in a shallow seashore pool at low tide?'

Well, I'm helping you to sort things out now. Some municipalities (not many) do provide these mini-learner pools, even if they are often labelled as mere 'paddling pools'. (The Trade calls them 'splasher pools'.) Still, paddling is a fair start.

Authorities that don't provide them should do so. And this is the rub. Education authorities without the benefit of shallow-water 'Learner Pools' are unlikely, even unable, to promote swimming with their youngest infant and primary school children.

So many of the conventional or standard-type pools provided are simply too deep for infants and a lot of older children as well. Standing shivering in chest-deep water isn't likely to encourage water-confidence and relaxed enjoyment with apprehensive youngsters. It most certainly isn't a sensible and practical approach to teaching them swimming and water-safety. This is what we and those municipal authorities must face up to. And not waste much more time, either.

These 'paddling', 'crawler' or 'splasher pools' are supplied by a limited number of manufacturers in the 'Learner Pool' business. It's all a matter of demand and economics. Most things are these days.

FIG. 2. *Cranleigh splasher pool. 12ft diameter × 3ft deep.*

DEPTH REDUCTION

Of course, there is always the possibility (or hope) of reducing the water depth down to 12in in the more standard beginners' pools of 3ft or so, to make it safer and suitable for infants.

This is done in some well-organised districts, especially where the infant and primary school has its own small indoor pool. They generally work on a Monday-to-Friday system. Start off Monday morning older classes in the regulation depth—say 2ft 6ins to 3ft, gradually reducing the depth of water from day-to-day, ending on Friday afternoon with the youngest learner pupils in the shallowest depth. This can be the 8in to 18in recommended for the absolute infant sinkers, or whatever depth is judged suitable—according to the teaching method used and the progressive imagination of the head teacher. Many heads think this complicates curriculum-planning too much and won't consider it at all.

This *depth-reduction* system depends largely on having a *small* indoor pool with a *minimum volume of water* to start with, what is known as the 'Classroom Pool'. And you certainly won't get this without first having a head enthusiastically convinced of the validity and practicality of the 'Shallow Water Method', and with the initiative and drive sufficient to convince his local authority. He will have to push them relentlessly. We may well know what we want: the difficulty in getting it may be frightfully frustrating. We mustn't weaken. It's mostly a question of educational economics. Just like life!

Probably what you need urgently, as a lever to exert special pressure, is a young mothers' group in your area, formed to persuade your local authority to provide the right sort of shallow water pool (if it's not told it may never know!). Isn't this all part of what you pay rates for?

Depth Reduction Difficulties: leaving educational idealism for practical fact, here are some strong reasons why a number of colleagues feel they must be wary of this shallow-water depth reduction method.

1. Difficulties with maintaining correct chlorination balance from day-to-day and controlling other bio-chemical fluctuations in a pool of daily varying depth.

2. Problem with disposal of large volume of run-off water—danger of flooding local drains or sewers. (With efficient chemical control and mechanical filtration, the same water could possibly be used indefinitely, so this accounts for reluctance to empty out most of the water weekly to put depth reduction into practice.) This is why you should have a *small*, minimum-volume pool.

3. Uncertainty of engaging a caretaker with sufficient know-how—or who is willing to put himself to a little extra trouble to make the system work efficiently. (On the other hand, most

school caretakers *are* wonderfully obliging and proficient.)

4. The necessity of having the right kind of headmaster (or mistress) who cares enough about the scheme to *want to make it work*. (He must have an overwhelming urge to want his young children to swim.) What is your's like?

5. Difficulty in getting enough money from your education committee to provide these extra facilities. This is really the bug-bear! (If your school has its conventional pool, then it needs its mini-pool too—as an essential part of its Physical Education programme.)

6. Then there is the possibility that the school's water supply is accounted for on a water meter. This might well cause reluctance to use 'excessive' amounts weekly. (Another good reason for the mini-pool.)

No doubt you can bring to mind other difficulties I have left out; but I don't want to get carried away! I'm primarily promoting swimming and water-safety, particularly for youngsters. No, that's not fair: for anyone of any age who needs help.

The point is, try not to be discouraged if there aren't these ideal facilities in your neighbourhood right now. Honestly, they are not out of this world.

THE OLDER LEARNER CHILD

This older child, pre-schooler or otherwise, still needs water shallow enough in which to stand up and move about confidently, comfortably and safely, waist-deep, or less, from both the psychological and temperature point of view. They won't be able to learn much or enjoy the teaching session in cold water. Actually, the recommended minimum temperature is generally stated as 85° F. For rank beginners, warmer water could be even better, perhaps a necessity, 90° F in this case.

We'll be reading how to use these regular 'Learner Pools' later on. The main thing is to be convinced that they are necessary, that they are the easiest and safest way of converting sinkers to floaters and gliders, that they actually are practical from a professional point of view (see special chapter 20 on the 'Classroom Learner Pool'), and that they are available.

Here are some successful leading firms in the 'Learner Pool' business:

Purley Pools Ltd.,
P.O. Box No. 132 Godstone Road,
Purley,
Surrey, CR2 2YQ

Clark Pools,
J. A. C. Kingston & Sons Ltd.
Upton Road,
Reading, Berkshire, RG3 4BJ

Mermaid Poolquip Ltd.,
Daux Road,
Billingshurst,
Sussex, RH14 9SN

Cranleigh Pools Ltd.,
Cranleigh,
Surrey.

SAME DEPTH OVERALL

Remember, your 'Learner Pool' must be of uniform depth from end-to-end. 2ft 6ins or 3ft is usually most practical, then it can be used for swimmers as well. You don't fill it to maximum for infant sinkers, so this requires special planning.

If your municipality has only the 'Olympic' type pool, with its 4ft 'shallow end' sloping to 10 or 12ft under the diving boards, now is the time to apply the pressure.

Form your parents' 'Learners' Swimming and Water-Safety Association', and work on your council to provide the 'Learner Pool' your children need—indeed, *must have*.

N.B. I haven't included details of pool management and maintenance because I don't think you want them from me here; but have made this brief reference to special aspects of the 'Learner Pool' for the record.

There is an enormous gulf sometimes between recommending what is theoretically or educationally ideal, and what in fact is actually practical and possible.

Some teacher colleagues for example, are particularly (and justifiably) sceptical about this shallow water depth reduction system. 'There are too many difficulties for it to work,' they say. (I think they enjoy listing them!)

Then maybe they write me off and struggle on with their well-tried if not exactly popular methods based on 40 children plus to an orthodox pool of deepish water—well, deepish to an infant. Whereas I know, sometimes I'm apt to push educational reform and smaller classes of half that number to permit greater personal care and attention. Not a new concept, we all know that.

CHAPTER TWO

The Home Pool

This need not be dismissed as the impossible luxury you may imagine it to be. Specialist firms provide remarkably available pools of simple, sectional construction to suit most modest incomes.

The chief difficulty is not in paying for them, but in having somewhere to put them. They are basically garden backyard pools designed to fit into (or on to) an average lawn or patio with minimum dimensions of 15ft × 20ft. (There are smaller pools, but you need room to move around outside them.)

Of course, they are outdoor pools, with use generally restricted to the warmer seasons. But one firm* at least does supply effective lightweight screens that retain extra warmth in the water and a more comfortable air temperature surrounding.

The point is, with suitable back or front garden space, you can

---

* Purley Pools Ltd.

have your own pool, and so be able to control its water volume and depth to suit the personal needs of your family. Then your children will have the learning conditions they need to overcome fear or nervousness and develop confidence and swimming ability during their most impressionable years.

Of course, the requirements for the domestic situation are different from those in school, obviously. The main difference is class instruction compared with individual attention at home.

Some firms supply nice little home pools, based on aboveground, sectional construction for ease of assembly. Yet they wouldn't stand up to the heavy day-to-day class load in school. So you have to sort out just what you need. It's not difficult.

Here's the sort of thing:

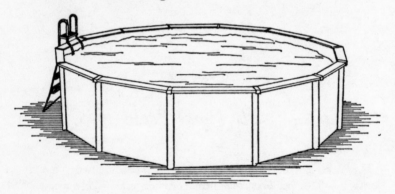

FIG. 3. *Home pool by Clark*

CHAPTER THREE

The Play Pool Complex

We've talked about shallow water pools to suit various ages and abilities. What every town and city needs is a *Play Pool Complex* combining these pools for all needs, plus additional features and landscaping to increase the effectiveness of swimming and water-safety programmes.

The emphasis should be on play and fun instead of formal competition. If space (and money) permits, the usual graduated depth training and racing pool should be included in the overall landscape design. Here is a summary of factors to consider:

(a) A play and learner pool complex for the whole family.

(b) Shallow splasher pools 12in to 18in deep.

(c) Small learner pools of up to 3ft in overall depth.

(d) Running water foot baths.

(e) Play fountains to wet faces.

(f) Play slides and water chutes to encourage fearless entry.

(g) Buoyancy aids and play equipment freely available.

(h) Professional teaching help and supervision constantly provided.

(i) Seats on benches (fixed) close by, so the child can leave the pool and be by its parent within seconds—for praise, comfort, encouragement, advice and for towelling.

(j) Refreshment bar for nutritious hot drinks and edibles.

(k) *Chief aims:* eliminate fear, increase water confidence and safety, benefit from instruction, encourage total family participation.

CHAPTER FOUR

Reaching Aids for Rescue

EXTEND YOUR REACH

The idea is to lengthen your reach by holding on to one end of an object like a pole, and avoid jumping into the water yourself to make a rescue. The R.L.S.S. in their book on *Life Saving and Water Safety* strongly recommend that a would-be rescuer should first consider two methods of rescue from the bank before attempting to enter the water himself; they are—REACH or THROW. This way, even a non-swimmer can be helpful. With poor or uncertain swimmers, jumping in hastily is often how double tragedies occur.

This is assuming you are called upon to rescue someone from the water in an emergency. Of course, if the person in difficulties was close by the bank or pool-side, no doubt your first reaction would be to reach down, grab hold and pull him out as quickly as possible, if you felt you were capable.

Even then, you would be wise to have something fixed and firm to hold on to with your shoreward hand—or have someone hold on to you. The object is to prevent one water mishap from becoming two!

However you choose to do it, the principle remains: when possible, you should avoid direct personal contact with the person in the water, and so you make use of a convenient object nearby to extend your reach. You also keep your centre of gravity low by lying on your stomach, sitting, kneeling or crouching while you reach out. As a beginner yourself, you can't afford to risk being pulled into the water by a panic-stricken sinker.

With this reaching aid method, even if you cannot swim at all, you can be of great assistance by extending your reach. You do not leave the safety of the bank, dock, shore, wharf or boat, and so your own life is not in danger. This is not selfish, it's sensible.

WHAT WITH?

No matter how small, every swimming area should have some rescue equipment handy. Reaching aids that should be standard equipment are: lightweight reaching pole (probably bamboo, with the ends padded and bound); 50ft of nylon or polyethylene heaving line (which does not get waterlogged), or 5/16in manila or sisal rope; ring buoy and similar heaving line, which is a more effective combination.

Additional reaching aids that may be available at other places where bathers gather: boat cushion, paddle, oar, towel, kickboard, plank, ladder, branch, belt or any article of clothing, even a light-weight chair, especially if it floats. The main thing is to have a mind that can recognise and utilise such objects

when someone is in difficulty in the water within your reach—
or extended reach.

Of course, your own arm is the most efficient aid, if the sinker
is near enough to be reached without you entering the water;
but remember, if you attempt to do this, you MUST always anchor
yourself firmly with the other arm to the shore or pool-side.
You must not take chances—assuming that you are a non-
swimmer, or a beginner. And even good swimmers are liable to
suffer water-hazards and drown. Maybe they take chances thinking they are immune to accident. Knowledge isn't much use
if it comes too late!

THE 'WARE' LIFE-SAVING APPLIANCE*

This is a light alloy device that is supplied to some County
Boroughs, Education Authorities and Urban District Councils
for their swimming pools. It is a tapered, anodised green tube
in four sections, with a 22in steel ring covered with neoprene
rubber and fitted with two floats for buoyancy. The pole is
capped with rubber, and the whole is supplied with either hook
or clip fittings for horizontal or vertical wall storage.

By having two, from 20 to 24ft long, one on either side of a
pool, most of the surface area can be reached from the side. If
a person is spotted in difficulty, the appliance can be extended
from the pool-side, and the ring placed accurately into his hands,
or over his head and shoulders if necessary, then he can be
drawn steadily and safely to the side.

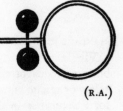

(R.A.)

FIG. 4. *The 'Ware' life-saving appliance*

* Ware Safety Appliances Ltd., Bowling Road, Ware, Hertfordshire.

(R.A.)

FIG. 5. *Reaching aids for rescue*

CHAPTER FIVE

Buoyancy Aids for Rescue and Learning

STANDARD EQUIPMENT FOR POOLS

The important thing is for all pools, public or private, to have buoyancy aids prominently located for instant use for personal safety or rescue purposes. There must always be something handy for a swimmer in difficulty to grasp and hang on to—but not another swimmer if it can be helped.

Torpedo Buoy: about 3ft long, of foam rubber and painted a bright fluorescent orange, this life-saving device was designed in America and has achieved a big advance in popularity with

34

lifeguards on both sides of the Atlantic. It might even supersede the old cork lifebelt. I don't think there would be many tears.

The buoy wraps around the chest beneath the arms with a simple snap fastening and supports the swimmer with his head slightly back and comfortably on top of the water. The buoyancy of this rather overstuffed sausage is enough for two and was first introduced to Britain at the 1968 Life Guard Corps convention at Blackpool, where it was enthusiastically received, particularly by officers of the R.L.S.S.

It is not a learn-to-swim gadget. It was never intended as such, but principally for the lifesaver who has to swim out to a bather in difficulties. When just beyond reach of the bather he can push one end of the buoy forward to be grasped, and so avoid the risk of being gripped personally by a possibly drowning man. Our policy exactly.

Being lighter and softer than the conventional cork ring lifebelt, this torpedo buoy can be thrown to a person in the water without fear of doing him an injury. It's certainly a most useful piece of safety equipment to have permanently by the side of pools, piers, river-banks and seaside promenades.

Swim Floats: most of us have seen these handy little swimming and training boards by now. We used to call them kickboards in Canada, but they have a variety of uses for both beginners and experienced competitive swimmers, so swim floats is probably the most suitable term (provided you don't confuse them with the entirely different arm-floats).

One attractive make* is from resilient urethane foam enclosed with PVC, in red, blue, green or yellow. Very durable, light and practical, in two sizes: *Learner Float* 16in × 11in × 1⅜in. *Training Float* 12½in × 9½in × 1¾in.

Another type is from Purley Pools Ltd., made of expanded white polyethylene, in one size: 11½in × 8½in × 1in, a neat, handy little float.

These floats are certainly very handy to have at a second's notice to toss gently towards a swimmer in trouble. However, they are mainly used as a buoyancy aid in learning to swim, and as a

---

* Sports-Link Ltd., 19 St. George's Sq., Huddersfield.

training device for strong swimmers who wish to become stronger, principally in the legs.

For these reasons, most public and school swimming pools have a plentiful supply ready to hand. (Of course, they're also more economical to purchase in bulk lots owing to their size.) They ought to be standard equipment.

'Swim-Easy' Arm Floats: these are, pure and simple, inflatable buoyancy aids for learning to swim, principally for infants and children. We shall be studying their use further on; meanwhile it's sufficient to say that as they have become so popular and successful, both privately and with school classes, many pools now have them readily available. They are a very handy little teaching and learning device, but not in the lifesaving sense of the buoys and floats. You don't throw arm-floats to drowning persons. But to help you to swim when you've imagined you're a sinker all this time, yes, arm-floats are for you. You'll be floating and swimming (after a fashion) in no time at all.

OTHER BUOYANCY AIDS IN EMERGENCY SITUATIONS

This is largely a matter of quick-thinking and commonsense. If a person is spotted in trouble in the water, then he needs helping, fast, but sensibly, whether you can swim or not. But you don't jump in and attempt to swim out to make a personal rescue. We've explained this before.

What you should do is quickly to look for floatable objects light enough to push or throw to the person in the water, to keep him afloat while you get help. (Assuming the standard lifesaving equipment we described is not available. Also assuming you are still in the beginner's class and so don't go jumping into the water after people.)

Suitable objects to look for: swimming ring, lifebelt, surfboard, short plank, empty petrol (gas) can, spare tyre, safety cushion, small wooden ladder, even a wooden chair. (Beach ball, although obvious, is not so good: it rides too high and catches the breeze, and is also difficult to grasp and hold on to.) I don't need to remind you that you don't throw these objects at a drowning person's head, but to one side for him to grasp.

I'm not suggesting you should expect to find all these sundries conveniently placed by a swimming pool (that's what the standard safety equipment is for). But it's just as well to have an eye for such things and to know how to make use of them in an emergency.

And remember, they not only can reduce the hazard for a struggling swimmer in difficulty, but for you personally, on the bank. This is the point.

P.S. I haven't talked about lifejackets up to now. Maybe I thought they were obvious and had been given enough coverage in other water-safety literature. It's true that every child and non-swimmer using boats, river banks, wharfs and waterside structures for work or recreation are urged to wear life-jackets as standard equipment.

This recommendation is synonymous with the wearing of seatbelts in road vehicles. It is a preventive measure. But the contrariness of human nature guarantees that both disciplines will be ignored by the majority, irrespective of statistics proving their usefulness. Most people would consider them just too much trouble, a nuisance and an encumbrance. But two wrongs don't make a right.

In our teaching context, lifejackets are not buoyancy aids for rescue or for learning to swim, but purely as a device for preventing a non-swimmer from sinking and drowning. They certainly are most unsuitable for learning to float, glide and swim, being too much of an encumbrance to free movement. Let us just acknowledge their usefulness in water-safety for certain conditions; but state their unsuitability for our purpose in learning to swim.

Coming back to swimmers: even they may owe their life to a lifejacket one day. So in certain situations where a swimmer is intimately associated with deep water, like sailing and other boating fun, he should seriously consider using a lifejacket. No one is infallible.

PART TWO

Simple Buoyancy and Propulsion for Pre-Schoolers

What being submerged totally in water means to you now depends upon how you were introduced to it as an infant, and what your intimacy with it has been like since. Although it's not too late to acquire an ease and a pleasurable skill in water, whenever you choose to start, the earlier the better. So the object here is to encourage adults to accept a responsibility towards helping the very young become safe and fearless swimmers—even from the age of six months.

CHAPTER SIX

Check-list for Success

(a) Arrange to take the lesson at the same time of day for each teaching session. Babies and young children like and are reassured by regularity.

(b) Regularity and consistency provides the healthy habit and rhythm of learning that makes progress and improvement easier.

(c) Short, concentrated, *frequent* teaching sessions are best. Ideally, one each day; three weekly should be the minimum.

(d) No meal, feed or drinking within an hour before the swimming lesson, or any active session in the pool. Let the inner man have his nutritional reward *after* the lesson.

(e) Water temperature for beginners, of any age: 90° F. Comfort and pleasure are vital at this stage. The lessons must be enjoyable.

(f) Depth of water most suitable for acclimatisation and water-confidence; a depth which will allow the beginner to keep his head comfortably above the surface while (a) he is sitting on the pool bottom, (b) touching the pool bottom with his hands while floating stretched-out on his front ('crocodile'). This is the 'Splasher' pool.

(g) Depth of water more suitable for the actual learning process (pre-schoolers): 12in, 18in, 24in to 30in are four ideal depths according to the age and size of the infant. Even the baby has to have enough depth to submerge and swim underwater. This will be the 'Learner' pool of variable depth.

(h) Allow junior playtime in shallow water before the actual teaching session, so he can get accustomed to the water in his 'own time'. He must associate you and the water with enjoyment and fun.

(i) Main aim: to build-up water-confidence and to avoid saying or doing anything that might introduce nervousness or apprehension in a child that initially had no natural fear of water.

(j) Do not attempt to teach the swimming strokes used in competition to the young beginner. Be content to progress as far as complete submersion, underwater and surface breath con trol: basic front and back float; simple gliding and rudimentary propulsion by flutter-kick and finning and sculling with the hands and arms on the back, and elementary 'Dog-Paddle' on the front.

(k) When this basic buoyancy and movement is learnt, both underwater and on the surface, introduce water-entry from the pool-side: (1) jump, (2) 'Stride-Jump' keeping the face above the surface, (3) plunge and glide ('torpedo'). The adult will be in the water to receive and support.

(l) You do not train your pupil to keep his head above water at all costs—which might seem to most people the logical thing to do, because then he would not be conditioned to under-water survival. Psychologically, you would be conditioning him to fear of underwater experience.

(m) Satisfy yourself instead that your pupil knows what to expect and *to do* when he finds himself underwater, maybe for the first time. Put him through the 'Golden Rule' again and again. MOUTH CLOSED, EYES OPEN, BRAIN ALERT, BODY RELAXED.

PARENT'S TEACHING TECHNIQUE

Although this section is primarily for the parents of very young children, and not a text for class teaching in school, a certain amount of teaching technique comes into it, naturally.

This is the key—*naturally*. The parent is unlikely to be pre-occupied with teaching ideologies and theories; simply concerned with giving her baby or infant opportunity for *total*, natural, water experience.

Instead of attempting to 'teach' separate leg, arm, body and breathing exercises as isolated, unrelated activities that used to be a popular swimming teaching method, she may quite naturally, fall in with current educational practice and provide this *total body* experience I mentioned. With young children, this is achieved most successfully through play-activity, albeit supervised and guided.

So here we have a non-professionally trained, non-teacher parent, nevertheless adopting a teaching method that is educationally acceptable—simply because it deals with the whole child and not just its separate parts. *It is providing opportunity for the whole child to gain its own learning experience.* We are not instructing the young child at this age, but helping it to learn.

This experience is acceptable to the child by being within the range of its comprehension and capability, therefore more effective. This is where the pre-selection of activity and sympathetic supervision by the adult is so important.

Then if the parent has a basic knowledge of swimming and water-safety, she can observe, guide, assist and add *progressively* to the child's advancement in water, even although it might happily imagine it is finding out for itself. This isn't an easy method, even although deceptively simple, and demands patience, understanding, sympathy, intuition and creative imagination from the adult.

THE PARENT'S ADVANTAGE AND VALUE

The parent will have the advantage over the child of having in her mind's eye a total picture of the 'finished product'—the subsequent objective: a child who can eventually swim recognised strokes. This she keeps to herself, to avoid suggestion of adult domination over the child in what it believes at this age to be purely a fun activity. She also would wish to avoid risk of the child's alienation, lack of co-operation and inevitable slow-down of progress.

The parent is unlikely to figure all this out for herself, being as we said, non-professionally trained; but it may well come to her intuitively if she possesses strong parental sensitivity. She is doing it all really, as any parent (human or animal) teaches their offspring—naturally, by conveying their own in-built experience in a suitably edited and scaled-down version. In this case, through play-fun activity principally of the water-confidence kind; not direct swimming instruction.

The main thing is, the parent has this mental picture of the child's subsequent advancement, along with the ability to guide the child towards it in a non-dominant, understanding, wholly sympathetic manner, controlled by a certain instinctive judgement.

Maybe I am pre-supposing here after all, that our nonprofessional parent has more teacher-ability than in fact she has. But then, it has to come. Being a parent is a complex learning process in itself: a mutual child-parent learning situation. That's what we're here for—to help both!

ONE THING LEADS TO ANOTHER

In the following chapters for the baby and infant, we are offering water-confidence activities acceptable to the child. And although they are presented as separate 'exercises' in this context, nevertheless are intended to lead to the child's acceptance of *total* water-experience (acclimatisation) as quickly and *safely* as possible.

Following that, we would expect the young child to advance to *total body* water-experience, unaided with its feet clear of the bottom by choice: 'Bouncing Ball' and other play activity; front and back float; gliding and elementary 'Dog-Paddle' both underwater and at the surface; water-entry by jumping and plunging. These in turn can subsequently develop into other rudimentary swimming movements and the main orthodox strokes as most older children and adults know them. But we're not concerned with teaching those just yet.

ONE FINAL NOTE

With baby in the water at play, the *horizontal* position is most important for getting the *whole* child to experience the ultimate swimming postures to come later.

Sitting and playing, ducking, bobbing and jumping are fine; but it is the *horizontal* position that will give baby his most effective, realistic experience of near-swimming, whether it be underwater or at the surface.

So get baby on his tum and on his back in water as soon as you can—kicking, splashing and making those first rudimentary, maybe instinctive, swimming-type movements.

This is encouraging the whole child towards total-body water experience free from fear in a natural sort of way—our chief objective.

CHAPTER SEVEN

From the Very Beginning: Waterproofing the Baby (Based on total submersion)

(P.F.)

FIG. 6. *Baby 'swimming' underwater*

The earlier in life the child is introduced to warm water on a total body submersion basis, the quicker, safer and more effective will be its acceptance of water as a natural element, free from tension or fear.

HAND IN HAND

Learning to walk and learning to 'swim' should go hand-in-hand. Both should be taught with equal care and attention.

Both need ever-ready encouragement, the reward of warm praise and a situation that enables the young child to experiment, explore and learn in its own way and its own time. But always the parent must be close to hand to maintain an atmosphere of reassurance and security. For the mother at least, this shouldn't be asking too much.

The baby, the infant, the youngster and so the adult, must have every opportunity to develop their experience of water as a genuinely friendly element.

The longer this is delayed, the more difficult to achieve is the child's tension-free acceptance of total submersion and fun-movement in water as a completely natural, thoroughly pleasurable activity.

IT STARTS WITH BATH NIGHT

There's no doubt, if the process is handled right, that the baby can quickly become acclimatised to water—via the bath tub. Before it is a year old, it can be floating, gliding and happily performing natural, instinctive-seeming swimming movements in the pool (if it's warm enough), with or without 'Swim-Easy' aids, but with of course, high quality supervision.

But please, don't run away with the misconception that you are making baby a 'swimmer'! At least, not the conventional, formal concept of swimming.

Two factors emerge if we wish to accept this thesis of acclimatisation as utterly feasible and practicable:

1. The first and foremost responsibility of every parent towards its child's ability to float, glide and 'swim', is thoroughly to *familiarise and naturalise the naked baby to total bodily submersion into water of a comfortable and enjoyable temperature —early in its life*. This temperature factor is vital.

2. Modern mothers have long been advised and urged to do this with their babies, under six months old, as a normal part of bath-time, as relaxed, fun-orientated, play-activity.

STEP-BY-STEP ACCLIMATISATION

(a) *Water play is fun*—if safety is always considered. You

understand about safety precautions, personally; but avoid making a fuss about them in any negative, fearful sort of way in sight or hearing of the child. Just carry them out, unobstrusively. Remember, you are wanting baby to develop naturally a *fear-free* attitude towards water, not a fear-inspired neurosis about it —like some of us still suffer.

(b) *The bath tub leads to the pool*: the splash and sensation of pleasurable water on naked skin; experience of buoyancy in water shallow enough to be safe and eliminate fear; the enjoyable sensation of voluntary body positions and elementary breath control. This comes from the calm acceptance of water trickling or flowing over head and ears, splashing on to face.

(c) *Position of baby's head* is the key for safety and to offset panic. Its neck muscles are weak and may not support its head above water unaided. But you must ask yourself, is this the chief objective—keeping baby's head above water? In fact, is it necessary? The truth of it is *no. Baby does not have to keep its head above water.* (Straining to do so is only *your* idea of swimming. It is not a necessity for baby.)

IN THE BATH TUB

(d) Get in with baby. (Is this too much trouble or impractical?) The whole point is you want to retain and develop his complete confidence. Babies perceive and register far more than you might imagine they do; so you must clearly demonstrate your own natural, fear-free water-confidence first—at least at the same time. (I can imagine this will kill the idea for a lot of mothers. Pity.)

(e) Fill the bath about two-thirds with pleasantly warm water. In you get with baby and a few floating toys. Sit him in your lap, supported, and play together. Let him splash and get his face wet. Encourage him to enjoy this little exercise, it is most important. Don't prolong it.

(f) With cupped hands, sponge or soft flannel, trickle water over baby's head and ears. Gradually include the eyes and increase the amount of water (suitably warm). Do this with him in both supported sitting and lying positions.

(g) Holding baby under the arms, facing you, dunk him up

and down in the water, playfully. As soon as you can see he likes having water on his face, (and why not, he hasn't discovered fear yet), submerge him *very briefly*. He will instinctively hold his breath under water. This is the start of it all—natural survival reflex.

(R.A.)

FIG. 7. *'I like water'*   *'This is fun'*   *'Nothing to fear'*

(h) Support baby on its front in the water, with your hands under chin and tummy. Let him kick and splash naturally. But be decisive about the submersion of his face. It should either be clear of the water so he can breath without effort or concern; or *totally submerged, nose* and *mouth*, so that he has to hold his breath instinctively. Never submerge just the mouth alone, as he may then attempt to breathe through his nose and suck up water.

(i) Encourage leg-kicking and arm movements while laying-out in the water, supported safely by mother's hands. Include the dunking as fun; but don't be in a hurry to repeat it if he seems upset by it. Return to the sitting and trickling water over the head until he is having fun again. *Never let opportunities for nervousness creep in.*

(j) Remove him from the water if he cries—straight into soft, warm towelling and affectionate cuddles.

(k) Get baby used to 'laying in' the water, fearlessly, then kicking its legs and making instinctive 'dog-paddle' arm movements. This can be done submerged, with your hand under chin and tummy. Lift baby's head clear to the surface so he can take a breath. Do this by *under-pressure on the chin*. Repeat so that he gets used to coming up for air when you press or lift his chin. It becomes almost a reflex.

(l) Experiment with baby in floating positions, both front and back. You start with full two-handed support, and gradually reduce it to a minimum. By this time, if he is old enough to sit alone securely, you will be outside the bath; but never must you leave him alone in the bath, or even outside it if the bath is full, while you leave the room for a second or two. Crawlers and toddlers can quickly get into unexpected trouble.

(m) Be generous with kindness and loving praise. Although baby won't interpret your actual words, he will recognise their warmth, affection and tone of approval. This is what he wants. He does understand differences in tone of voice and your facial expression, so a smiling face is essential. I'll remind you again: a baby perceives more than you might imagine.

BUT WHAT ARE YOU LIKE?

It is a baby we're talking about, under a year old. Now a baby isn't born afraid of water; it's what you do with it or to it in water that decides its fear or fun.

This doesn't imply that we shouldn't do anything at all—for fear of failure. Waterproofing baby is an essential part of its early education. We have a duty to try.

Of course, if you are hopeless with babies and children, a fumbler and bumbler, easily irritated, quick-tempered, quicker with a smack than a loving word, maybe the baby would be better-off if you left the learn-to-swim stage until later-on—after it can walk and talk.

Even then it might be wiser to hand-over to a professional. Some parents are just no good at all at educating infants—either not caring enough, or too impatient, or simply not having the knowledge. Well, is this little bit of information going to help?

It's entirely up to how you feel, how you see yourself in the role of teacher. In fact, at this stage, you're not really teaching baby—simply providing the happy, fear-free opportunity for him to explore and discover for himself, with the vital aid of personal parent involvement. *This is the real point of it.*

NEXT STEP THE POOL

We've got about as far as we can go in the bath with baby, short of actual swimming. Remember, we are *not* trying to keep his head above water. To do so is only to introduce fear (which is foreign to him at this stage, until you introduce it—and you're trying not to do this, aren't you?)

We want baby to be fear-less, to accept water naturally, to love playing in it, gliding through it, being *under* it.

You can see, it requires a fresh way of thinking, a new approach by the parent. We are not dreaming of teaching the crawl, breast-stroke, or any formal swimming stroke allegedly popular for class instruction. These are preoccupied with keeping the face above water, as if that is the chief criterion in learning to swim. It isn't. We want baby to feel happy, comfortable and confident with his face and head *under* water. It means really, have *you* the nerve to try?

I'm not pretending that what I'm proposing now is original or unique. Others have done it successfully. It is entirely in line with contemporary educational thought and practice. My aim is to increase its range. I'm just suggesting we try it.

WATER TEMPERATURE

This should be established before going any further. Not that you'll always get what you want in someone else's pool; but you are in charge of your own bath tub, and the water there needs to be tepid to be comfortable and pleasurable.

For swimming pools, 90°F is a recommended temperature for learner pools. You can't afford to let your raw beginners get chilly. They won't thank you for it, nor be in a hurry to repeat the experience.

Many public pools are kept below 80°F. I suppose it's all a matter of economics. And of course, it depends too upon the use to which they're put. Swimmers, particularly in training, don't want warm water, it's too enervating; they prefer to be briskly stimulated. The humidity of the atmosphere has a lot to do with this. So a well-managed pool must have both suitable water temperature and surrounding air free from excessive humidity. This means an air-conditioning plant.

From the Very Beginning: Waterproofing the Baby

I appreciate that all this is not exactly your concern. You're not in the business of pool management. But whether you are a teacher or a learner, you still need to be knowledgeable and selective. It's just as well, therefore, to have these working temperatures stored away in your mind for reference.

Anyway, remember that the baby, infant or child does not move about in the water energetically enough to maintain his warmth by his own efforts, as a swimmer in training will do. So it's your responsibility to keep him warm and comfortable.

1. Be selective in your choice of pools to get the right temperature. Or if you're out of luck here—

2. Keep the actual lesson-time short and snappy. And don't forget that big, soft, warm bath-towel and lots of brisk rub-a-dub-dub!

A LITTLE WATER-BABY

Baby is going to make natural, instinctive-seeming movements *under* water, once you have both got through the acclimatisation process. This hinges on total submersion—after he has successfully gone through the first stage of getting his head, ears and face wet, and enjoying it. This means the eyes too, of course. Initially, he'll blink them shut reflexly. Later you'll teach him to open them under water quite unconcernedly. (You'll do this with the aid of large, coloured, plastic poker chips).

1. Baby sits on mother's lap on the pool-side, or better still, on the pool steps in shallow water for his first lesson, securely supported, but able to kick and splash, and make pulling or pressing movements through the water with his hands. It is also most useful if baby can observe other small children playing in the water.

2. Baby is taken into the water, *held in mother's arms*. But swim caps, ear plugs, nappies and nick-nacks are quite unnecessary and even hazardous. The naked body is ideal; but a pair of soft swim trunks can be used if you feel happier with them! He won't care one way or the other. Just make sure they don't bind, cut or chafe.

3. Both mother and baby should wear their same suits for each lesson, for familiarity—important to baby, to avoid dis-

51

traction. He needs the reassurance of instant recognition.

4. Play at dunking baby under water, just a split second at a time, facing each other and together. Be lavish with warm praise when you come up. Even one such dip per lesson may be enough in the early stages.

5. Let baby get the feel of laying in the water on his front, supported under chin and tummy. Move him through the water to trigger-off the swimming reflex.

6. The movement-strokes baby makes at this stage should be similar to his movements on the carpet or in the cot. A natural, instinctive crawling action with alternate limbs, or maybe with both feet and legs together, frog-like when he is very young. This is what we want him to do in the water. No attempt to teach any form of orthodox stroke, please.

7. Try him on his back too, supported under head and waist (but make sure you shade him from sun or glaring lights by positioning yourself thoughtfully). Move him along; but no submersion from the back-float.

8. Now introduce the coloured poker chips. First in the shallow water of the steps, getting baby to reach out and pick them from the surface as they float, while you hold him (if he can't yet walk). But let him walk towards them if he can.

9. Increase the length of submersion time, from the brief split-second dip, to longer periods of one, two, three, four seconds, and more if he shows no fear or discomfort. You are doing this with him at first, facing each other, and encouraging him to look at you under water by smiling and waving.

10. More practice at opening eyes under water by using the poker chips on the steps. He will have to go under and reach down to get them. *Lots and lots of praise every time*.

11. Include this underwater practice in the bath tub, making a game of it. This will be a daily practice, as against perhaps two or three sessions a week in the pool.

12. You are now moving baby along *under* water, supported under chin and tummy, but letting him kick and press or pull freely with his hands and arms. Gradually reduce the two-handed support until you are guiding him towards you up to the surface by his chin alone. This will be so he can take a breath. He should be able to stay under without distress for five

seconds or more. Shaking his head is a sign he is needing air; but you have to guide him to the surface by his chin so he can get it.

(R.A.)

FIG. 8. *'I see you!'*   *'I want one'*   *'I can reach'*

13. You are working towards the moment when you can release baby *under the water* completely *before* guiding him to the surface. By this time he should only need a gentle pressure under the chin to bring him up; or simply a gentle tap with your fingers. You are trying to teach him a 'breath-recovery reflex'—how to come up towards the light and the surface for air.

WHAT ELSE IS THERE TO DO?

Baby isn't a swimmer yet, not by a long way. But you have established a most important principle: he can submerge and move under water independently—and enjoy it. While you are close at hand to observe, guide, help him to recover for air, and praise him warmly when he does.

You are both being educated to understand that baby doesn't have to be afraid of being under water. At this stage of under a year old, there is none of the panic-stricken straining to keep on the surface. Baby is as much at ease under the water as on top of it, (unless you've done something to spoil things for him).

There are further stages of progression, naturally, with or without buoyancy aids. You will also want more information on these aids, and of course, about learner pools. We'll get to them.

But for now let me say, I do understand I have been asking a lot of you. Not every mother is willing and ready to give as much care and detailed attention as I have proposed.

She may not even be able to swim herself. Perhaps she has a pathological fear of water. But every mother (or dad) can spend the time on bath night with baby. Maybe they can take it in turns. So at least we can progress that far. Try. P.S. Use praise for reward, not sweets.

You can see, this requires a mother, or father, to care a lot and to give freely of their time. Is this too idealistic for many (most?) families? We must be realistic. Am I asking too much?

It is obvious that what I have outlined requires the personal, loving approach. This acclimatisation of baby is not for the class instruction method. If you can find neither the time nor the pool to do it this way, then baby will have to wait a few more months —for other swimming aid. Don't worry, it can still work out.

SUMMARY OF LEARNING

(a) Start early: from six months to six or seven years. For the child, the earlier the better. Learning to walk and to swim should go hand-in-hand. This is based on the *total submersion* method. There is no attempt to keep the head above the surface initially.

(b) Acclimatisation should start in the bath, with mother joining in. Water temperature should be warm, comfortable and pleasurable.

(c) Trickle water over baby's head and face as an enjoyable sensation, leading-up to complete submersion for a split-second. The underwater time is gradually increased—keeping the experience pleasurable fun. This is both mental and physical conditioning (page 47).

(d) Float baby on front and back with two-handed support (page 48).

(e) Encourage natural arm and leg movements in horizontal floating positions.

(f) Reward baby with warm praise and affection for his efforts. He is remarkably perceptive (page 49).

(g) Try a warm, shallow-water pool at this stage (not less than 90°F).

(h) Baby is not expected to keep his head above water during this learner stage, but to feel perfectly comfortable and happy underwater as a natural element (page 50).

(i) Opening eyes underwater is taught with the aid of large coloured poker chips, or their equivalent, both in the bath and pool (page 51).

(j) Increase length of submersion time by going under with baby to show and reassure him. Gradually reduce your two-handed support to one-hand chin guidance on his way to the surface (page 52).

(k) Release baby completely underwater before guiding him to the surface (page 53).

(l) *Objective so far*: encouraging baby (or infant) to do natural, swimming-type movements underwater—the 'Dog-Paddle'. (Formal strokes are *not* taught.)

(m) *Length of lesson*: 30 minutes maximum, depending on temperature, fun and interest.

(n) *Frequency*: once a day, ideally; three times a week minimum and regularly. Consistency is most important.

(o) Portray affectionate patience at all times. Baby's water education cannot and must not be hurried. You must avoid saying or doing anything that might set him back psychologically. To help baby to swim, *you* may have to learn the art of kindly approval and warm encouragement.

CHAPTER EIGHT

Swim-Time with Crawlers, Toddlers and Infants (Total submersion plus natural *buoyancy*)

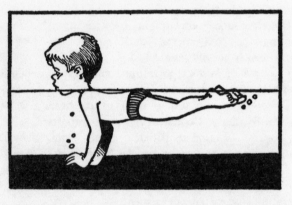

(P.F.)

FIG. 9. *Playing 'Crocodiles' and blowing bubbles*

If you don't do anything to introduce apprehension and nervousness, there's no reason why junior shouldn't take to this method like a duckling. He was born without fear of water until an adult put it there. So we've a lot to answer for.

A DIFFERENT APPROACH

Firstly, you have to make up your mind how you want to tackle this learn-to-swim problem with the very young. We've had a good look at it from the baby's angle. By starting early enough before it had a chance to discover fear of water, we went straight in with the *under-water natural method*. This demanded total submersion and a disregard for buoyancy in the initial stages.

This probably asks more of the parent than it does the child! Well, we are asking the parent to go into the water with the child, and then there is the almost instinctive shrinking from 'risking' the child under water. I know this is asking a lot. So it's little wonder there aren't more takers.

IT'S YOUR CHOICE

I must emphasise again: individual intimacy and total involvement is our method: not impersonal class or group instruction. How do you feel about that? If you're not up to it, here's what you do: (1) forget the whole idea, hoping that somehow or other he'll be taught to swim well enough at school. 'It's not my job...' sort of thing! (2) find a professional or someone you can trust to take on the job for you. But it's got to be someone *baby can trust too*. Someone who loves children and whom children quickly get to love. Otherwise all three of you are in for trouble.

We better see now what can be done to please both sides.

NO EASY WAY OUT

With the help of a simple buoyancy aid, the *arm-float,* we'll have junior take to water like a duckling all right. But don't run away with the idea that this means goodbye to all that difficult under-water business. We're going to run both methods simultaneously. For any success, we must, whether the adult likes it or not.

So from now on, it's going to be persuasion, training, conditioning, self-discovery and lots and lots of practice to master two basic water arts: *total voluntary submersion*, and *buoyancy* (either natural or aided).

BACK TO ACCLIMATISATION—AND THE BATHTUB

1. *Water is for fun:* lots of face-wetting, fun-ducking, bubbl-

ing, splashing and gurgling. We're working up to something.

2. I better let you in on it now. It's all to do with this seeming paradox of submersion plus buoyancy. We have to get junior to accept as *entirely natural* his ability (or tendency, this early) to submerge and 'swim' under-water while holding his breath (eyes open eventually), along with the new experience of floating at the surface, maybe making swimming-type movements (propulsion), and discovering that's the place to breathe.

3. It's a joint exercise of combining these two activities, seemingly contradictory, yet essentially compatible and mutually dependent. This is the turning point of our efforts—success or failure.

4. Junior will accept them as natural enough, as long as we don't do anything to change his mind. Let's do our best not to transfer our inhibitions and nervousness to him. Please.

5. *Blowing out:* so far, baby has been holding his breath under water, surfacing to breathe, with a little guidance from mother's fingers under his chin. This is purely an introductory exercise to get him to accept submersion, getting him waterproofed.

Very soon, he will have to float, glide and paddle about at the surface and stay there, happily, breathing more or less normally. So we now start teaching him to *exhale under water*—to blow bubbles. Holding the breath can cause tension, and we're not training him for skin-diving.

6. *Breathing in:* making bubbles in the water will make blowing *out* under the surface a habit. Breathing *in* is instinctive, so don't make a fuss about that. When the lungs are emptied, it's natural to take a breath. But you must show him initially the direction in which to breathe—where to come up for air, by gentle pressure under his chin after he has made the bubbles. (You must be right there.)

7. *Being an oyster:* more advanced bathtub work. Breath is taken just above the surface, *through the mouth*; face and head then totally submerged to lay cheek on bottom of the bath; release air bubbles *through nostrils*, like an oyster, before coming up for more air. Unless he has a stuffy nose, head cold, asthma, or whatever. In which case he wouldn't be able to release enough air through his nostrils and so might feel panic. Don't push

this underwater play while his nose is blocked-up.

8. *Whales and submarines:* you can't expect babies and toddlers to know what these are; but getting junior to play whales and submarines at this stage in the game is all to the good. You know how these creatures and vessels operate. They're dependent upon air, but can spend a comfortable long time under-water with the air-supply they take in on the surface. (This is still self-discovery bathtub practice; but equally suited to the swimming pool, so we'll get back there soon.)

WASHBOWL FUN

A standard exercise: this might be for an older child (the infant under 7), maybe not. Fill a plastic bowl two-thirds full with warm water, place on chair or floor. Junior lays face in the water, blows bubbles through his nostrils. *Turns* his head, not lifts, to one side, keeping one cheek on the water, breathes in through mouth, turns face back into water, exhales through nose as before. Lots of repeats. He can add any sound he cares to make under-water through his nose without opening his mouth, using his head as a sound-box. It adds more fun. If he can't release enough air through his nose, then he uses his mouth as well.

Opening of the eyes under-water is an essential part of the exercise. So bring in the coloured poker chips again, or something similar. And don't forget to reward his efforts.

TO SWIM OR NOT TO SWIM?

Are you getting impatient and thinking, 'What's all this to do with swimming?' Or, 'When are we coming to the swimming bit?' Don't worry, we're getting there. But it's junior I'm considering.

Our approach is entirely from the grass roots (or should it be seaweed?) I'm not even thinking about actual swimming yet—not the orthodox strokes anyway. I hope you're with me.

Some folk aren't. For example, a teacher friend commented, 'I think you're too optimistic. I don't see how you can expect any child under five to learn swimming properly...' I interjected swiftly, 'What's properly?' She replied, 'You know, front crawl, back crawl, that sort of thing...'

Ah, now this is the crux of it. I'm not recommending these orthodox strokes for the pre-school, infant non-swimmer at all. I'm dead against it. I'm concerned purely and simply with introducing the sinker, non-swimmer, learner, beginner—whatever label you like—to water so they will take to it without nervousness, tension, fear or inhibition. They must be happy, confident and at ease in, under and on top of the water.

I want them to be ducklings, mermaids, water-babies, tadpoles or tiddlers, able to disport themselves on or under the surface with equal pleasure.

But I don't want, nor expect, them to swim the crawl up and down the pool, just for the sake of pleasing an ambitious parent, teacher or club leader. Our approach is entirely different. That must be obvious by now.

The *individual* teaching method in this context is essential, not conventional class teaching. You may say, what authority would be willing to pay a swimming coach to teach one child at a time? It's not economic! What public pool could provide the necessary space, warm water and relaxed atmosphere? We're not short of problems!

There are countless children, adults too, who are either scared of entering water, or will be. They need help to overcome this introduced fear and to become swimmers. But in the sense of being waterproofed, drownproofed and danger-free. This is not synonymous with swimming the crawl, breaststroke, butterfly or dolphin up and down a pool. This is club stuff. It's outside our range altogether. Let's not get preoccupied about that.

Now back to the job in hand. We've got those toddlers to turn into tiddlers.

IN THE SWIMMING POOL

Now all our mutual efforts in the bathtub should pay off. We should have an infant by now who is indifferent to getting his face wet—who genuinely doesn't care whether his head is under or above the water. It should be all the same to him.

We have done nothing to arouse any feeling of apprehension;

but everything to condition him to experience a happy glow of achievement, mental and physical, whenever he has voluntarily gone under water, blown bubbles there, surfaced to breathe and submerged again. A kind of natural cycle. (And incidentally, this is very close to drownproofing.)

Remember, he has surfaced expecting our warm praise and evidence of affection. Even babies are perceptive enough to expect and notice this.

CROSSROADS FOR BOTH OF YOU

This is it. The big decision. Are you going to continue with the step-by-step build-up of his confidence without any buoyancy aids at all? Or shall you switch over, as it were, to the *arm-floats* stage?

The arm-floats will keep his head and face completely clear of the water, and his body near the surface all the time. This is a complete reversal from what we have been working-on so far.

Because it seems contradictory, will it destroy his natural confidence and ease under-water? Will it cause conflict? Is this new concept of mergence between submersion and buoyancy ridiculous?

Answer: not if you handle it right. You are not going to do away with his underwater ability, but add another skill to it: the skill of floating and surface propulsion.

So hand-in-hand you are going to develop his natural underwater play with the very first stages of surface swimming. (No. No crawl yet. Forget it.)

IT'S UP TO YOU

Now please bear with me, because I must round-off the progressive sequence of the natural method with mother (or father) and child, before taking you through the arm-floats method.

It's like this: if you prefer to continue the in-with-mother, personal, natural tuition without artificial aids, and you have the time, inclination and ability, please have a go. You'll probably both have lots of fun and thoroughly enjoy yourselves. What could be nicer? This is what it will entail, in the pool:

(a) Lots of underwater play—both of you.

(b) Mutual dunking up and down; getting those eyes open, both of your faces to smile—underwater.

(c) Gradually getting junior to experience horizontal floating, front and back, with minimum support under chin or head.

(d) Transferring his rudimentary '*Dog-Paddle*' underwater, to dog-paddle propulsion on the surface.

(e) His neck muscles may still be a little weak in proportion, so watch his head. (Underwater this was no problem; but he's on the surface now and you must accept a slightly different responsibility for his breathing.)

(f) Continue with the minimum chin support with your fingers, if needed for him to breathe.

(g) *On his front* he'll be doing a half float, half dog-paddle type movement; resting his head down between his arms if his neck feels tired, and blowing-out through his mouth and nostrils. Raising his head with your guidance under his chin, just sufficient to breathe. And so-on.

(h) Don't insist he strains his head back continuously. We're trying to eliminate tension.

(i) *On his back* he should be practically floating by now, with your minimum support under his head. He'll probably do rudimentary kicking and flipper-like arm movements too—the start of propulsion. Not that he'll know it!

But steady-on! Here's how you get him to this latter stage.

CRAWLERS INTO 'CROCODILES'

1. *In the bathtub:* have junior play 'crocodiles' in water shallow enough to let him touch bottom with his fingers, while his legs and body float to the top. This is the start of him learning to keep his face above the surface to breathe normally. At the same time, you still keep encouraging him to submerge and blow bubbles. *He must maintain this skill.*

2. *In the learner pool:* more 'crocodiles' in shallow water; and of course, a sandy, seaside beach on a warm, summer's day is ideal, especially if there is a shallow pool left by a receding tide.

This is the mergence of those two basic water arts—submersion and buoyancy. It must happen naturally and easily. It must be fun, apprehension-free, and he must love doing it. It's just play. While you know it's fun-learning.

3. *Unaided floating:* ('going to sleep' on the water). Have junior stretch out on his back on the water: ('Lay your head on my hand and go to sleep...'). To assist the horizontal position say, 'Make a big tummy...' This should straighten-out his back for the floating position. Maintain fingertip contact for reassurance.

4. *'Bouncing ball':* face each other in the shallow end, holding both hands. Junior jumps up and down off both feet, progressively higher and deeper, finally submerging completely—with breath control. This is where the previous bathtub play at 'whales' and 'submarines' pays dividends. By now he should be offering no resistance at going under—nor should you!

5. *Floating and gliding:* tow junior about the shallow end. More 'whales' and 'submarines'. Then, while swimming on your back with a gentle flutter or frog-kick, with junior on his back too, grasp him along both sides of his head over the ears in front of you at arm's length, tow him along. (He'll be just above your thighs.) Pretend you're a tug-boat. Have him flutter his legs and fin his arm too. ('Be a fish.')

(R.A.)

FIG. 10.   *Washbowl breath control.*
'I'm a bouncing ball'

JUMPING AND PLUNGING

He should have all the trust in you he needs by now, and all the confidence in himself. So it shouldn't be difficult to persuade him to take the next step—or jump.

1. *Jump and catch*: from a squatting stance on the pool-side, he jumps outwards towards your outstretched arms as you stand waist-deep in the water. Catch and lower him into the water simultaneously. Repeat if he reacts to it as fun. Each time let him deeper into the water as he lands, relying less and less on your arms. Also jumping from an increasingly upright stance.

2. *Stride jump*: show him how to do the 'Stride Jump' entry, keeping the head above water all the time. Then it's his turn to show you. You are there in the water to encourage, but not to catch this time. This should be really fun. You will recognise it as the 'life-saving jump' entry to keep your eyes on the subject struggling in the water.

3. *Plunging and gliding*: once he has mastered the two jumps, and has no qualms at submerging briefly (while you are there to provide moral and physical support), demonstrate how to plunge in from the pool-side. This is total commitment.

Semi-squat stance, arms forward, head lowered on to them. Thrust off from the edge, plunging forward in a flattened-out glide like a 'torpedo'. If this is too much all at once, have him push and plunge in a semi-flat entry—hitting the surface with his knees and tummy first, with you there to catch and support.

Work-up to a full, unsupported, streamlined plunge and glide with extended arms. Then, add the flutter-kick for propulsion. You can just support his hands with your fingers if he prefers, and tow him along in the glide, until it's time to breathe. We mustn't overlook this. He might need a little chin support again.

(R·A·)

FIG. 11. *'Watch me jump!' 'I'm a torpedo'*

FINAL COMMENT—FOR THIS SESSION

Now you are both getting somewhere. Keep the experience fun. His age-group learns best through play.

Never slacken your alertness. He must never lose his faith in you or confidence in himself because of some carelessness or minor accident or unpleasantness. *You are the key to his progress.*

Positive praise and encouragement, always. Never negative or deflating remarks. Your praise is his regard, his constant reassurance that you care. We all need someone to care!

Be alert for him getting colder. Shivering and blue lips are a reminder you have over-done the water session.

Come out immediately, wrap him in that large, soft towel and make drying fun.

This flexible, fun approach gives junior the opportunity to discover how his body behaves; how best it can float, move through the water, go underwater and come up again, easily.

The child will accept it as fun and pleasure, if the parent (or teacher) sees it the same way, and has the desire and ability to make it so. So much rests with the adult.

ONE MORE THING

I know I promised the arm-floats this time. It's not that I forgot them. I wanted us to work our way through these other sequences first. It is best to get them sorted-out and it's good experience. But I'll bring out the floats next time.

SUMMARY OF LEARNING

(a) Personal involvement and individual attention by the adult is required for success.

(b) Underwater (total submersion) method still practised. Buoyancy awareness being introduced.

(c) Work towards combining these two main water arts; submersion plus buoyancy—as a joint exercise (page 58).

(d) Introduce exhaling under water: 'blowing bubbles'. Re-

D

duce previous practice of holding breath underwater—to avoid tension build-up (page 58).

(e) Do not over-emphasise breathing-in, let it happen naturally, instinctively. But do show the infant initially the direction in which to breathe by guiding his chin (page 58).

(f) Continue with more advanced breath-control in the bath-tub and washbowl: play at being 'oysters', 'whales' and 'submarines' (page 58).

(g) Breathing-out underwater, lifting and turning the head to breathe in, and learning to open eyes underwater are now taught and practised together in the washbowl (page 59).

(h) The 'crossroads' are reached. Question is: are you to continue the natural, progressive sequence of teaching without any artificial aids; or do you feel the need at this stage to use the help of some buoyancy support?

(i) Who needs buoyancy aids most, you or your pupil? (page 61).

(j) Shallow-water fun (bathtub and learner pool) playing 'crocodiles' (page 62).

(k) Unaided floating on the back ('going to sleep') (page 63).

(l) 'Bouncing ball' to develop underwater confidence and to *like* submerging (page 63).

(m) Water-entry from the pool side: *jumping and plunging* (page 63).

(n) *Jump and catch*: from a low squatting position, push-off and jump towards adult in waist-deep water, ready to catch and support.

(o) *Stride jump* entry: trying to keep head above surface.

(p) *Plunge and glide* from pool-side like a 'torpedo'. Add flutter-kick for propulsion. It is a small progression to lift the head and include the 'Dog-Paddle' arm stroke. Then the pupil is surface swimming.

CHAPTER NINE

Floating, Gliding and Propulsion with Buoyancy Aids

(P.F.)

FIG. 12. *Floating with confidence*

So far we have been occupied with waterproofing babies and infants before they start school—and this was directed chiefly to parents. The way I've done it might even bring criticisms of trying to get you to teach them swimming the 'hard way' without artificial aids—now that such things are invented. (A predictable reaction from some folk.)

However, I'm sure you see the underlying reason for waterproofing baby the way we have. Even if you haven't started with baby that early, the principle of developing water-confidence (and doing nothing to destroy it), and happy submersion with buoyancy awareness, applies to junior just the same. Or to anyone.

THE PROBLEM OF THE OLDER CHILD

If baby has become an infant before being introduced to water (other than for washing and drinking), getting him to accept it naturally and fearlessly may be more difficult, owing to the inevitable 'fear factor' intruding, even if unintentionally, during those early impressionable years. The baby after twelve months and throughout infancy, has had more opportunity to be exposed to this fear factor, and to develop inhibitions because of it. (Who would have introduced it?)

If you have waited until he is a child before acclimatising him to total submersion and natural buoyancy, *simultaneously*, you mustn't be upset to discover that he may not be as easily converted as I suggest.

Don't worry. The problem is not insurmountable. It's just that we will probably have to approach it a little differently— while still maintaining our submersion plus buoyancy principle as strongly as ever. We must never lose sight of this.

MENTAL CONDITIONING

The ability to float and swim is very much decided psychologically (submersion certainly is). Wooing this mental factor and building on it is more important and effective than simply wrapping a floating device around a person's arms to keep him on the surface without a mental decision on his part.

However, I agree, in the case of some 'hopeless' non-swimmers, that starting them off with arm-floats may be the only practical way. (It's a kind of reversal of our waterproofing method with babies.)

You have to assume that the older pupil, by using the buoyancy aid method first, will be led to the discovery that there is nothing to fear at the surface (because he can stay there with no trouble at all). He may then be persuaded to complete his water education by subsequent submersion. It can happen. It must.

A person is certainly not a truly safe swimmer until he can voluntarily submerge underwater for a period of time of his own choosing, as happily as he can swim on top; or, accidentally falling into deep water, can re-emerge without panic and remain calmly at the surface.

Starting a young child with arm-floats or a buoyancy jacket, without prior (or simultaneous) conditioning in *voluntary submersion* (waterproofing), can be like erecting a wooden fence without first rot-proofing the posts. You have an illusion of security, but no guarantee of permanency.

You can get youngsters to paddle around at the surface with arm-floats in no-time flat. But ask yourself: what is their mental (psychological) reaction to water *without* buoyancy aids? How would they react to total submersion (accidentally, say)? Would they be willing to do it voluntarily, and enjoy it? This, after all, is facing up to reality. Anyway, who says that swimming is only a matter of keeping at the surface?

EVIDENCE OF THE PROBLEM

A teacher friend told me about two of her young pupils. She had this little girl doing quite nicely on the surface, beginning to float, paddle about a bit. Then one day little Mary accidentally slipped off the pool-side and submerged.

Teacher got to her quickly, being an alert type, and pulled her out—'rescued'. She told me: 'Falling in like that set Mary back quite a bit...' (The psychological factor.)

Then there was Tommy. 'He can swim strongly the length of the pool, both front and back crawl, and also tread-water confidently; but is petrified at the thought of jumping into the deep end.' (Has he a phobia about submerging?)

'Ah, this is my point exactly. Take Mary: presumably she was instructed in floating and surface swimming techniques first, a formal procedure. But supposing she had first been waterproofed by submersion instead, then introduced to buoyancy and surface swimming as a follow-up? How could she have been "set back" as you call it? She wouldn't have had cause to be scared by accidentally going under, because she would have developed pleasure at submerging, free from apprehension. She would also have known the basic underwater survival technique.'

My teacher friend shrugged. 'That's your theory. But I'll allow you have a point there. One of my young pupils is the son of the pool manager. He could swim underwater like a fish before he could swim at the surface. In fact, I had a difficult job getting him to swim on the surface at all! He seems to prefer it underwater. I don't think he'll ever make a good swimmer. His crawl stroke is terrible. His balance all wrong.'

Never mind. You can't win 'em all. So, this young fellow probably won't make the school swimming team. But oh boy! . Is he safely waterproofed! Isn't this precisely what we're after with the pre-school child?—or anyone?

AT ALL COSTS

I wasn't trying to score points off my friend. She is a good swimming teacher, well informed on the latest methods, as well as being professionally trained in the conventional ones. It's simply that she wasn't able to have the right kind of pool to teach sinkers and learners in. (The Council wasn't providing proper 'Learner Pools'.)

This one was too deep for the purpose. Therefore most teachers who brought their classes there, thought they had no choice but to get their pupils swimming about at the surface, with or without floats, as quickly as possible.

As far as some children were concerned, what lay under the surface might just as well be a mystery world. To many, it certainly was a frightening one—but not to the pool manager's son!

I must say it. This policy, popular with many teachers, of getting pupils to stay at the surface 'at all costs', with or without floats, does not necessarily pay off in the long run. It can fail to introduce and familiarise the learner child with an enjoyable underwater experience. It can create a subconscious phobia about submersion. 'I must keep my face above water! I must! I must!' (The anguished cry of the potential drowner.)

What, you may well ask, would happen to the child if he fell into deep water without the aid of a float or a lifejacket? Say, from a boat, a pier, promenade, edge of a gravel pit, dock-side, slippery wharf, or river-bank?

I had to put forward this point of view. I wasn't going to recommend buoyancy unreservedly without a strong note of caution. I didn't intend leading you 'up the garden...' with any idea that arm-floats, kick-boards, rings or whatever, were cure-alls, even if they are most useful in developing *surface confidence*.

Don't forget, this is only fifty per cent towards personal water-safety.

NOW FOR THOSE ARM-FLOATS

They are two-chambered, inflatable, coloured P.V.C. arm-bands, slipped on the upper arm just above the elbow. They are popular, practical and cheap, therefore are standard equipment at many pools, for school classes mostly, and are sold at large stores and sports shops.

You could say they are ideal for by-passing or short-cutting the more commonly-used methods of getting the non-swimmer to float and dog-paddle at the surface with a confidence he lacked previously. Many teachers and swimming instructors think they are a God-send.

When you are responsible for a large, mixed class of young, nervous beginners, and you only have them once a week for about twenty minutes actual water-time, any aid that gets most of them into the water and paddling about at the surface willingly, is going to be a boon. You don't stop to worry about any possible sub-conscious back-lash this short-cut method may have later on. Or do you?

You've got most of them 'swimming' at the surface—a credit to your ability, and that's the 'proof of the pudding ...'.

This is just the start. Arm-floats don't teach them how to swim, that's the teacher's job. They are an aid, not a substitute for the teacher. Nevertheless, they are a great help, and most certainly safer and more effective than the former rubber rings. which were never considered really safe anyway. These arm-floats are safer, in fact, than any buoyancy aid that can easily float away from, or drift away with the learner-swimmer.

USING THE ARM-FLOATS

1. *Infants, children or adults:* the twin-chamber design has

two purposes: (a) a safety factor in case one chamber should deflate. (b) As the learner gains confidence with the floats, and begins rudimentary swimming movements, one chamber on each arm can be deflated, subsequently releasing air from both chambers. Finally, removing the floats altogether. 'You're doing fine Paul. Now how about trying the same thing without the floats?'

This way the beginner doesn't get too dependent upon the floats and is quickly given opportunity to try his own unaided ability. With a good fifty per cent or more pupils, this progression is fast. They are keen to have a go on their own, as soon as they discover their ability to float and dog-paddle with the arm-bands on.

2. *Babies:* arm-floats can safely be used with a baby as young as six to eight months, but in the bathtub first of course. They will support him in a semi-vertical position, with the head above the surface, the face clear of the water. (Is this how we wish to condition baby's fear-less acceptance of water? Remember our previous psychological submersion approach.)

So they are fine for keeping baby at the surface, in a kind of imposed float—if you wish to be excused the personal responsibility of waterproofing him naturally. Or if you felt you haven't the ability.

Once baby realises he can stay at the surface with these floats on his arms, will he become reluctant to submerge and get waterproofed the natural way? You both could have a problem!

Supported by the floats this way, baby will float and bob about in the water safely enough. He will also be able to do instinctive bicycling-type leg movements—the start of the dog-paddle. Alternatively, he might float more on his back and kick and splash with his legs. But he won't be able to do much with his arms. You can see why.

Look at the illustration and note that because the floats cover most of his arms down to his wrists (when they are normally meant only for above the elbow), they practically immobilise his arms for 'swimming' purposes. So we musn't expect the same 'swimming'-type advances with baby as we most certainly can with the older children.

However, arm-floats do provide floating confidence and encouragement free from fear in these early stages. Very useful indeed for parents who wish to get their children enjoying swimming pools at the earliest moment. Perhaps *single*-chamber arm-floats for babies is the answer, to permit freedom of arm movement.

A word of caution. The parent must always be close to hand and alert, constantly checking to see that baby's head doesn't fall too far forward and submerge nose and mouth, even if he can blow bubbles by now. *Arm-floats are not a substitute for the parent.*

(R·A.)

FIG. 13. *Baby with arm-floats*

N.B. You are left with the problem of deciding what form of water-introduction and instruction you wish your baby or infant to have in view of what has been said in previous chapters. But you know I don't wish to discourage you.

SWIM-FLOATS (OR KICK-BOARDS)

These provide valuable buoyancy aids for beginners, and for swimmers too who want to use them to gain extra leg-beat practice. Lighter than cork, non-dangerous and manoeuvrable, they are freely available at many pools, and teachers make frequent use of them in one form or another. Here are some practical ways:

73

FIG. 14. *Front glide and leg-beat*

FIG. 15. *Back float, glide and leg-beat*

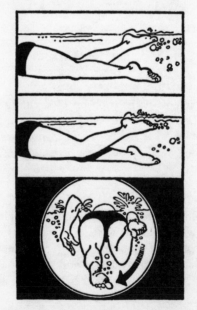

FIG. 16. *Leg action: on the front*

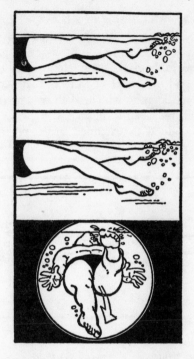

(P.F.)

FIG. 17. *Leg action: on the back*

1. *Leg-beat* for both front and back propulsion is identical, with just a differing emphasis on the upward or downward kick by a slight bending of the knees.

2. Relaxed 12in to 18in leg-travel, legs kept close together in passing.

3. Movement starts from the thighs, toes slightly turned-in.

4. Ankles remain flexible with whip-lash action.

5. Loose, relaxed 6-beat leg action with continuous rhythm.

6. Make the water boil continuously.

7. Avoid splashing on front or back (splashing is wasted power).

8. *On the front:* keep the seat near the surface. Knee bends slightly on *upward* kick, straightens on *downward* kick. Heels just break surface.

9. *On the back:* avoid 'sitting in a bucket'. Keep knees below surface. Knee bends slightly on *downward* kick, straightens on *upward* kick.

The pupil should hold the float along its sides or near its bottom corners and not clutch it from the farther end with his arms over the top. Soon he will need to become independent of the float and will be asked to push it away, either on his front in a 'torpedo' glide with extended arms, or from his back-floating-gliding position.

(P.F.)

FIG. 18. *Trying without*

(P.F.)

FIG. 19. *Why not two floats?*

These swim-floats are a most practical aid at whatever stage—beginner or advanced.

SUMMARY OF LEARNING

(a) The earlier you start with the child the better, the idea being that the later you leave it, the more chance the child has to develop fear of water and other related inhibitions.

(b) Having started the *total submersion* method first with the *young* child or baby, without any artificial aids, you can subsequently use buoyancy aids to speed-up his experience of floating, gliding and rudimentary swimming.

(c) If the child has grown older without gaining water experience, and therefore is probably apprehensive or even fearful of submerging and swimming underwater, teaching him first to float, glide and swim on the surface with buoyancy aids, may be the most suitable method.

(d) Hand-in-hand with the buoyancy aid method with the 'neglected' child, to gain his acceptance and confidence, you should include plenty of practice of face-wetting, eyes open and blowing bubbles underwater, and all manner of underwater confidence practices. This can be done in the bathtub, the washbasin and the paddling pool at home, in the school or town learner pool, and at the seaside. The activities must be fun.

(e) The child's experience of buoyancy (floating, gliding, dog-paddle, etc.) on the surface, must proceed *simultaneously* with his acceptance of underwater experience (total submersion). They should be associated naturally in the child's mind for his subsequent water-safety.

(f) This form of elementary waterproofing can then develop into essential drownproofing (page 68).

(g) *Arm-floats* can safely be used with the young baby or older child if for some reason you are either unable to teach the natural, unaided method, or don't wish to do so (maybe too apprehensive to try) (page 72).

(h) Although these floats safely support the baby on the surface, and allow him to kick and splash and do bicycling leg movements, they do restrict his arm action (page 72).

(i) As the child gets accustomed to floating and kicking on the surface supported by the arm-floats, the air can gradually be released from the separate chambers, thereby allowing the child to use his own physical resources to keep afloat, while still psychologically supported by the presence of the arm-floats.

(j) Don't overlook the fact that even when the child has learnt to become independent of the arm-floats entirely, he has still to be conditioned to accepting *underwater* experience. (You see, the floats were keeping him at the surface and so depriving him of this underwater experience. This could be their disadvantage.) (Page 72.)

(k) *Swim-floats* (or kick-boards) are for the older child, as they require conscious holding and manipulation for certain effects (page 73).

(l) They are very good for learning and practising front and back glide with leg-beat (the flutter-kick for the crawl strokes later on).

(m) From the start, the pupil must accept that floats are only aids, and that he will have to become independent of them eventually (page 76).

(n) Two swim-floats, one under each elbow, can help the pupil get more practice of floating, gliding and propulsion on his back. But the body must be *extended*—stretched-out.

N.B. These functional floats as described, are safer and much more practical and useful as learning aids than floating toys, rubber rings, air beds and beach balls. DON'T CONFUSE THE PURPOSE AND USEFULNESS OF THE TWO DIFFERING CATEGORIES.

COMMENT ON PART TWO

Just to confirm with you how far you might be expected to progress with these young pre-schoolers.

You aren't attempting to turn them into little orthodox swimmers and divers. Simply to encourage their fear-free acceptance of water to play about and 'swim' in, at the surface and underneath.

Most important, you want them to become safe in and around water, from as early an age as both you and they can manage.

The earlier the safer. They shouldn't have to be left 'till Primary School' before being taught how to swim.

To achieve this water-safety, they must be *waterproofed* by learning to perform elementary movements and breath control both *underwater* and at the surface, plus basic buoyancy awareness—unaided as a natural experience.

If they are old enough to understand and respond to actual teaching, and can interpret your physical and verbal 'lessons', then they may be capable of practising for and taking a simple 'Beginner's Swimming and Water-Safety Test'. (Part Three.)

It is worth trying and would certainly waterproof them most effectively—and add considerably to your peace of mind.

This is as far as you would expect to go with these under-school-age youngsters. Although by all means, if they show ability and willingness, and you feel capable, take them on further. Introduce the other variations and activities in Part Three—or some of them. See how they go. But remember, if you can make a start while they are *under* a year-old, *that* is the ideal target to aim at.

SPECIAL NOTE

Please don't think that I am being contradictory by promoting both *total submersion* and surface *buoyancy*. Much as it may seem that these cancel each other out, they are in fact strongly complimentary and mutually dependent.

You must have realised by now that our chief aim is to condition a baby, child or adult to complete acceptance of pleasurable, voluntary *underwater* experience, along with the ability to remain at the surface, relaxed and at ease an indefinite period of time—by choice.

This is true water-safety and our objective above all. It is in the achieving of these two fundamental experiences that you must be imaginative, enthusiastic, flexible and courageous.

PART THREE

The Older Non-Swimmer, Child or Adult

Floating and swimming is like learning to ride a bicycle; once you've learnt how you never forget. It should always have been part of you like eating and sleeping. And you know how much you like that.

CHAPTER TEN

Another Approach

WHAT IS A NON-SWIMMER?

A person of any age who is unable or unwilling to submerge his whole body, including head, voluntarily, completely under water with eyes open and stay submerged by choice without tension or fear; who cannot float unaided at the surface in any position, or move himself through the water by simple arm and leg movements, with feet clear of the bottom, preferably in a horizontal position. And finally, who is unable to breathe without strain while floating or 'swimming' at the surface.

HOW TO BECOME A SWIMMER

Expressed in terms of what is necessary to become a swimmer (beginner class):

1. Completely submerge underwater with eyes open.

2. Stay submerged by choice, with full awareness of the surroundings, until deciding to come up.

3. Float at the surface, on back or front in a position to permit breathing without strain.

4. Propel the body through the water by elementary arm and leg movements: on front, 'Dog-Paddle', or back, finning, sculling, or elementary backstroke.

5. Tread water unaided at the surface with minimal effort by arms and legs, permitting breathing without strain.

6. Or, stay at the surface by the 'Drownproofing' technique.

This is all elementary stuff. No-one is going to win any races by being able to do just this alone. You wouldn't be very safe out of your depth either, unless you were very confident and your 'Drownproofing' technique was trustworthy. But it is the barest minimum requirement to be a swimmer—of sorts. Achieve this and you will have overcome the first psychological hump— that first mental barrier. *This is important.*

As we are only concerned with 'beginners', we have to gain their confidence and persuade them to have a go at a set of very basic, elementary practices, with our help. They need a firm lead.

Alternatively, they might like to try in the company of a buddy. Perhaps they could learn together. But most certainly, never, never should a non-swimmer attempt any of these practices by himself. I don't have to spell it out? But I will, in Chapter 14.

WHO DOES THIS SECTION REFER TO?

Not the baby or infant. They were dealt with another way, and in some ways they have the edge over the older non-swimmer. But here we are up against *anyone* who can't swim. If it's junior just started school, or a water-shy aunt with a persistent phobia about sinking and drowning—that's all right. We are talking directly to them.

Both cases must have practical help. They aren't going to learn on their own, except perhaps one or two basic water-confidence exercises at home. Washbowl practice most certainly.

So I'll talk direct, lay it on the line. It is up to you to interpret these practices, either for yourself, personally; or to use and help teach a junior to swim.

WHERE DO YOU EXPECT THIS TO LEAD?

Work through this PART THREE, with a partner; use instructional help if you need it. You missed the boat as an infant, so don't expect to be molly-coddled now. Just work at the progressive activities in the water with a clear, sensible attitude. By the time you arrive at the end of this section, you should be 'Drownproofed', safe in and around water, and a different person entirely where water is concerned. You'll know 'where you're at', as they say.

This will leave you to study up the various methods for learning the standard strokes, have a go at practising them, and decide readily enough which one you can concentrate on first. For one person it will be the front crawl, for another the breaststroke, or the sidestroke. It just depends upon what suits you, particularly where breathing is concerned.

CHAPTER ELEVEN

Getting Used to the Water

IMMERSING THE FACE

1. From four to six inches of luke-warm water in a washbowl, scoop water up into your face with both hands, splashing it on to the eyelids. Repeat many times.

2. Inhale a medium breath, close the nostrils between fore-finger and thumb, dip your face into the water, right under. Hold it there several seconds then come up; but don't rub the eyes, just blink away the water clinging to the lashes. Practise often until it feels natural.

3. Now do the above without holding the nose. To avoid getting water up the nostrils, create air pressure in the nose to counter the water pressure outside. Do this by seeming to blow out through the nostrils, without actually doing so. This creates the inner pressure and the water cannot enter. Aim to hold your face under water for several seconds, easily. Try it with eyes closed, then open. Don't rub them.

4. Do the above plus releasing air through the nostrils as your face enters the water. Practise blowing out slowly through· the nose under water. Come up for air and repeat. Do stop-n'-start breathing under water—gain full control of it, ('motorboat breathing'). Now release air through both nose and mouth to-gether.

5. If you still have difficulty in opening your eyes comfortably under water, practise reading the printing on a penny on the bottom of the bowl. Put the face under with eyes closed, then slowly open them to identify the penny.

6. Round-off the exercise by inhaling through the mouth with the head turned sideways and one cheek on the surface, exhal-ing through the nose and mouth underwater by turning the face downwards fully into the water again. This is your regular home practice.

(P.F.)

FIG. 20. *Creating air pressure in the nose.*
'Motorboat breathing.'
Breath-control above and below the surface

ENTERING THE WATER AND ACCLIMATISATION

1. Starts with the washbowl practice, and submerging most of the body, head and face in the bathtub as well. It is helpful to do this by taking a medium-breath, then lowering the body and head on to the bottom of the bath, laying the cheek on the bottom and releasing the air under control from nose and mouth. Come up for more air and repeat. Become fully acquainted with and indifferent to water on the eyelids. Blink excess water from the lashes.

2. With a partner, the moment has to come for entering the swimming pool—shallow end. An over-all depth, shallow learner pool is preferable. At this stage, cautiously feeling for the bottom with the feet while wading-in is a sensible routine, just as you would with any strange body of water.

3. Once in, get acquainted with the water as soon as possible, getting the face wet, a bit of splashing and fooling about, ducking and generally getting the feel of the water as a pleasurable substance.

4. For the face and eyes, repeat the washbowl and bathtub practice, with the same breath-control. Try opening the eyes underwater—it has to come sooner or later. Although the eyes shouldn't be rubbed if the water discomforts them, lightly running the fingers and palms down the face from forehead to chin will remove the excess water. Anyway, you have to learn to be indifferent to this very minor discomforture.

Getting Used to the Water

5. Bobbing and breath-control is a good practice for getting used to the water. Keeping the feet on the pool bottom all the time, with a partner, bend the knees, lowering and submerging the body underwater. A medium-breath is taken above the surface and exhaled beneath the water as previously practised at home. This exercise can be done simultaneously so that both partners are underwater together, or with a see-saw effect. With both persons underwater, they can open their eyes to observe each other, smile, pull faces, etc., note the release of air bubbles.

(P.F.)

FIG. 21. *Bobbing and breath-control*

EXPERIENCING BUOYANCY

1. *Jelly-fish float:* the most effortless float to do, with a partner to note the results and assist the floater to his feet afterwards. Here's how: standing in waist/chest-deep water, feet apart, take a medium-breath, slide the hands down the legs towards the ankles, letting the head droop forward underwater. Keeping

the arms and legs straight but relaxed, the feet will leave the pool bottom, the body will rise exposing the rounded back at the surface. Hold the position in a relaxed, droopy fashion with the limbs as 'tentacles', until ready to be assisted upright by partner. The breath is *held* in this exercise.

2. *Recovery from the float:* sooner or later this has to be done

(P.F.)

FIG. 22. *Jelly-fish float*

(P.F.)

FIG. 23. *Recovery from front float*

unassisted, but the partner is there for all the practices. This is a two-part technique: (a) lift the head and tuck the knees up. (b) Sweep the hands backwards towards the hips and straighten the legs downwards, feeling for the pool bottom with the feet. Stand up.

3. *Front float:* easily performed from the jelly-fish float. Simply extend both arms and legs horizontally towards the surface and hold this position relaxed. Partner is ready to assist floater to stand-up.

Another method is for the partner to support the floater initially on his front and gradually remove the support.

Try to increase the time of the floating position.

4. *Back float:* bend the knees, crouch down until water is over the shoulders, with partner supporting the back of the head and neck, slide backwards and extend the limbs and body along the surface. Keep the hips well up, the head back, arms by the sides—and hold the breath until the float is established. Partner is there all the time to assist—and to gradually remove his support of the head and neck.

5. *Recovery from the back float:* a two-part technique similar to the previous recovery. (a) Lift the head, tucking the chin down and bending the knees. (b) Circle the arms backwards, downwards and forwards up past the hips, pushing the water with the open palms towards the feet, at the same time bend at the waist and straighten the legs downwards to feel for the pool bottom

(P.F.)

FIG. 24. *Recovery from back float*

with the feet. Stand-up. Partner should be right there to assist this recovery.

TOWING AND GLIDING

1. *Towing:* working in pairs, take it in turns to tow each other through the water in front and back glide positions. On the front, the towing is done from the outstretched hands; on the back it is done by placing one hand under the floater's shoulders, the other hand under the head and towing him gently backwards. Support should gradually be reduced to a minimum.

2. *Front glide:* face partner, a little distance apart, in the learner pool. Crouch until the water laps over the shoulders. Take a medium-breath, extend arms along the surface, thrust-off, dropping the head down on to the surface and glide to partner, keeping body extended and streamlined. Hold breath until standing-up again. Do it like this and there's no reason to fail (unless it's psychological).

3. *Back glide:* with back to partner, crouch and lower the shoulders beneath the water. Medium-breath, lean back into the water and thrust off backwards into a glide towards partner, keeping arms by the sides, the head back and the hips up to the surface. This will achieve that necessary stretched-out body-shape. Keeping air in the chest cavity will create buoyancy. Support from partner or swim-float is helpful at first.

TREADING WATER

An important resting skill to learn as soon as possible. It could well come in now, after getting used to the water, floating and gliding.

Treading water is simply relaxed, vertical swimming in one spot, putting out just enough energy to keep the head above water to look around, get your bearings and make decisions. Here's how to do it.

1. In chest-deep water with a partner and a swim-float (two would be better). Even a pair of arm-floats wouldn't be amiss at first.

2. Supported by the swim-floats under the arms, raise the feet from the pool bottom and work the legs as if riding a bicycle or climbing stairs. Do it energetically enough to give you the feeling of support.

3. Experiment with the 'scissors-kick' and the 'frog-kick' also, and use the style which gives the best results. But aim to make the kick slow and relaxed (you are supposed to be conserving energy).

4. Now bring one arm into use, while still supported by a swim-float (or the pool side, or the reaching-pole held by your partner).

5. Both arms perform a wide-spread, circling and pressing action just below the surface. By pressing down they keep the body up.

6. Ready to try it in deeper water? Have your partner give you gentle support under the armpit with the reaching-pole.

7. Lean forward a little into the movement, to create more resistance to the water.

(P.F.)

FIG. 25. *Treading water*

91

RELAXATION—WIDE, SLOW CIRCLING AND PRESSING WITH THE ARMS—
SLOW, RELAXED SQUEEZING AND TREADING WITH THE LEGS—CALM,
REGULAR BREATHING.

Have your partner standing-up at all times to help you out of
any difficulties.

CHAPTER TWELVE

Elementary Propulsion

After getting wet all over, opening the eyes underwater without
difficulty, floating and gliding happily, a person needs to feel
he is in charge of his own body in the water. He wants to make
it go, to travel under his own power. He realises he has power
available, if he only knew how to use it effectively.

Our concern is to teach him how, not for speed, but for easy,
relaxed *safe* travelling through water. We want him to feel
confident, safe and resourceful wherever he chooses to use water
for his recreation and exercise. Having got used to the water by
now, he should be ready for a little bit of easy learning about
strokes. Here is what we recommend.

(a) *Gliding and flutter-kick (front and back)*: the easy,
rhythmical, six-beat leg action can be practised on land from a
reclining-sitting position. RELAXED, FLEXIBLE LEGS—TOES POINTED
DOWN AND SLIGHTLY IN—STEADY, EVEN, RHYTHMICAL LEG-BEAT—
12in TO 18in LEG-TRAVEL—WHIPLASH ANKLE ACTION.

Get it going in the water—most probably a swim-float would
help more than anything (along with a partner). Refer back to
Chapter 9 on buoyancy for use of the float in front and back
glide positions. Keep the kick fairly slow and shallow to start
with, until the motor muscles of the legs have become accustomed to the vigorous exercise.

(b) *Finning on the back*: short, neat wristy arm action while
gliding on the back. Starting with arms at the sides, draw both
hands up to the waist level about 6in from the body, flexing the

wrists and opening the palms towards the feet; then close the arms to the sides, pushing the water downwards towards the feet as the hands close into the thighs.

Try to cover the intervening distance to partner by use of hands only in this fish-like, finning action.

(1) Keep the head well back, the hips well up.

(2) Breathe evenly and normally, avoid tension.

(3) Let the legs trail straight but relaxed.

(4) Include the flutter-kick with an even, relaxed rhythm to co-ordinate with the finning action.

This is the simplest form of self-propulsion on the back.

(c) *'Dog-Paddle' on the front* (the 'human stroke'): an easy, natural, elementary 'crawl' on the front; reaching with alternate arms from the shoulder just beneath the surface and pushing downwards and backwards with the hands to propel the body forward while keeping it up at the surface.

(1) At the beginning, keep the head relaxed in the water to avoid strain; raise or turn it to breathe when necessary.

(2) Exhale underwater, raise and turn the head sideways to breathe in (take a 'bite' of air through the mouth); relax the head back into the water.

(3) Trying to strain and keep the head up out of the water all the time distorts the body position and makes the leg action difficult.

(4) When this arm-action and breathing comes easily, include the flutter-kick to co-ordinate with the dog-paddle.

This is the nearest thing to the more advanced 'Front Crawl'.

(d) *Sculling on the back*: similar to finning, with a fuller arm action producing more power. Both hands are rotated away from the sides as the arms are separated from the body and drawn upwards and outwards, bending the elbows; then squeezed back towards the body pushing the water with the palms towards the feet. So it is a squeezing-pushing propulsive movement, with flexible wrists.

(1) Keep the head resting back in the water.

(2) Breathe normally without strain.

(3) Keep the hips up to the surface.

(4) When the sculling arm action produces definite movement, include the flutter-kick and improve the joint stroke.

This should be a relaxing, non-tiring form of travel.

(e) *Elementary Back Stroke:* a graceful, relaxing, resting stroke, permitting full, normal breathing. On these merits it wins over the 'Front Crawl' as one of the earliest swimming strokes to learn—comfortably. It begins and ends in the back gliding position—streamlined, encouraging an easy, loafing action. The ideal stroke when there's no hurry to go places.

The arms and legs have a *recovery* and *drive* action, like a frog, with the glide coming at the end of the drive.

Glide   Recovery (*1*)   Recovery (*2*)

Drive   Glide

(P.F.)

FIG. 26. *Elementary Backstroke*

94

RECOVERY

As the legs are drawn upwards and outwards and opened, frog-like, draw the thumbs up the sides as far as the shoulders, keeping the elbows tucked-in. Then extend the hands and arms sideways ready to pull and drive just beneath the surface, no deeper.

DRIVE

Squeeze and snap the legs back together, frog-like pushing against the water with the soles of the feet, holding them together for the glide. At the same time, sweep and pull the wide-stretched arms back to the body, pulling with the palms, squeezing with the inner arms. Hold them at the sides for the glide.

1. Inhale with the recovery stroke.
2. Exhale forcibly with the drive.
3. Bend the elbows slightly on the pull for more power.
4. Maintain the glide position until momentum is nearly lost.

There's no doubt about a person being a swimmer with this attractive stroke.

(f) *Adding power to the backstroke:* in the recovery action, continue drawing the hands up past the sides of the head, keeping the elbows tucked-in. Stretch the hands and arms close together up beyond the head into a streamlined spearhead. Then with elbows slightly bent, sweep the arms back down and around through a 180° arc to the sides of the body, snapping the legs shut at the same time—and glide. This is as much power as you can expect from the stroke.

(g) *Frog-kick, a whip-kick?* The term frog-kick was used just now thinking it would be more easily understood. But with modern-day instructors, this 'old-fashioned' leg action is no longer good enough, advancing with the times and developing into the *whip-kick*. It should be described so you know what's going on, although no-one will blame you for sticking with the good old frog-kick.

(1) Legs straight and together (glide).
(2) Bend knees, drop feet downward (still together).
(3) Part the feet and circle them away from each other, mostly a lower-leg action.

(4) Snap and squeeze them back together, pushing with the feet, and glide again.

This is a narrow, more restricted action than the former frog-kick, using mostly the *lower legs* and not the wide-open thighs —so it doesn't look like a frog-kick any more; but has this whip-like, snapping action of the lower legs, ankles and feet.

It can cause difficulty for the beginner, confusing him with technicality, instead of allowing him to perform an easy, in-stinctive frog-kick (even if it isn't so effective).

So in the learning of this 'Elementary Backstroke', try not to get too technical over the leg action. Do what comes natural at first. Refining and correcting can come when the total stroke is being done reasonably well. Don't worry about it just now.

CHAPTER THIRTEEN

First Beginner's Test

TO ADVANCE FROM NON-SWIMMER

These are a few basic, minimal practices you must expect to master together.

I'll set out the test first, then explain each item for you to learn.

FIRST BEGINNER'S TEST (Basic minimum)

Water confidence, buoyancy, propulsion, water-entry.

1. Submerge head and body completely by squatting in waist-deep water (6 seconds).

2. Bobbing and breathing rhythmically (6 times).

3. 'Jelly-fish' float (10 seconds).

4. Front glide and stand up. (Swim-float permitted during practice.)

5. Back float (30 seconds), stand up. (Swim-float permitted during practice.)

6. Front glide with flutter-kick (20 ft). (Swim-float permitted during practice.)

7. Front glide into 'Dog-Paddle' (20 ft).

8. Back float into finning or sculling with the hands and flutter-kick (20 ft).

9. Water-entry (1) jump (2) plunge and glide from squat stance.

EXPLANATION OF TEST

Carried out with partner, parent or teacher in the water to participate for safety's sake, encourage and test the items. Partner communicates when test times or distances are achieved.

1. Standing in waist-deep water facing partner. Take a medium-full breath, bend the knees into a squatting position underwater with eyes open. Hold this underwater position for six seconds. Exhale through mouth and nose (let it flow out), straighten-up and breathe normally above surface.

2. Standing as before: breathe in through mouth, bend knees and submerge into squatting position, exhale through mouth and nostrils; straighten-up and inhale through mouth, bend knees, submerge and exhale as before; repeat rhythmically six times. Permitted to hold hands with partner during practice to overcome nervousness. 'Bobbing and breathing' is included here as a *water-confidence* activity, not an exercise to learn breathing for the front crawl. You'll learn *that* by doing it when the time comes.

3. Standing as before: inhale medium-full, bend at waist and tip gently forward to float face-down with rounded back and arms and legs hanging relaxed. Hold for ten seconds then stand up and do recovery-breathing.

4. Standing as before, holding swim-float with both hands along its edges: inhale medium-full, reach and tip forward, pushing with feet off pool bottom into stretched-out front glide. Stand up and do recovery-breathing. Practise with float until able to do it unaided.

5. Standing as before, holding swim-float in front: bend knees,

lean and tip backwards, stretching-out body into back float, with swim-floats held relaxed at surface just over lower belly and thighs. Back of head and neck fully in water; legs as near surface as comfortable (but permitted to droop relaxed). Hold for thirty seconds, breathing normally. Stand up. Practise until able to do it without swim-float.

6. Adopt position with swim-float ready for front glide: medium-full breath, thrust forward into glide with leg-beat action (flutter-kick), avoid splashing. Do twenty feet, stand up and do recovery-breathing. Practise until able to do it unaided.

7. From standing in waist-deep water; inhale medium-full, thrust forward into front glide, lift head until chin is at surface, 'Dog-Paddle' with hands. Hold breath if you wish at first; but try to exhale and inhale above surface without strain. 'Swim' this way twenty feet, stand up and do recovery-breathing. Add flutter-kick. Now try to *ex*hale below surface, *in*hale above.

8. Go into back float with stretched-out posture: move both hands and lower arms into easy 'finning' stroke, *pushing* the water down towards feet, streamline recovery-stroke. Include easy flutter-kick. Develop this arm action into 'sculling', bringing in upper arms too. *Propulsion stroke*: pushing water with hands towards feet, squeezing action of arms to sides of body. *Recovery stroke*: easy, streamlined. Leg-beat continuously with easy, six-beat rhythm, toes turned-in, ankles loose. Travel twenty feet, stand up and recover.

9. (a) Standing on pool edge ready for jump entry. Practise from bent knee, or squat position to be nearer the water at first. Try both double-foot and single-foot take-off, springing well out to avoid bumping against side of pool.

(b) Squat on pool edge, arms forward: thrust and plunge outwards towards surface of water. Strike and glide like a 'torpedo', face down between forward-stretched arms. Stand up and recover.

COMMENT

These 'beginner's' practices will give you the water-confidence and buoyancy awareness you need to develop your swimming ability and increase your enjoyment.

Work through these and you're no longer a nervous sinker; but a person eager to learn more water skills and become a good swimmer of different strokes. You should by now be hooked on the water.

Study the rest of this PART THREE, it's all for you.

CHAPTER FOURTEEN

Supervision and the 'Buddy System'

Apart from the fulltime, professional pool manager-come-instructor, who is employed to take care of every aspect of pool management and use, supervision is the unrelenting responsibility of every person in charge of children—even if it is a bore me saying so. But I'd rather be criticised for that, than accused of ignoring it altogether.

Unsupervised children in or near water are a hazard. I know we shouldn't need reminding; but accidents are happening each year in open water because children are being left to themselves.

Gravel pits, river banks, lakes, canals, farm ponds, wharfs, pleasure boats and sea-sides are areas of hazard to young children; but not necessarily so if they knew what to do when they hit that water surface and went under for the first time. Or better still: if they had competent supervision. But here we are back to failings of human nature. Supervising children is such a drag to some people, that they find something else to do. Or maybe they have some kind of misconceived faith.

SPECIAL RESPONSIBILITY

Teachers with their swimming classes, parents with their own youngsters, accept this responsibility with the sixth sense of their calling. Don't they?

A person might get away with loafing on the games field and let their class get on 'doing their own thing'; but although free play and free practice is perfectly allowable in the swimming lesson, nevertheless, the teacher's keen eye roves continuously over the group, observing, noting every individual quirk and characteristic, alert and ready for every eventuality. This is what we believe, anyway. We want it too.

The children's safety and their lives are both our personal and professional responsibility during every second they are in or near water.

And it's no use saying this is all a bore because it's been heard so many times before. We are never going to escape the moral and physical liability of this one. Anyone want to? All right, preaching's over.

PAIRING-OFF

Do this and you'll have the comfort of knowing no-one is on their own in or near water. This applies to the small family group, the youth club's trip to the sea or lake, the school party on canoeing instruction and every swimming lesson in school time.

EVERYONE WHO GOES SWIMMING, BOATING, CANOEING, FISH-
ING OR SHRIMPING SHOULD HAVE A PARTNER

Try to pair-off according to age and ability. Each swimmer should have a water-buddy of his own class or grade. Beginners go with beginners; active swimmers go with partners who can match them in skill, output and interest.

Beginners need moral and physical support from each other; swimmers want to have fun and competition with their own kind.

Buddies can be paired-off afresh at the start of every swimming session, or selected on a permanent basis at the beginning of the season, whether it be for the school term, or summer camp.

BUDDY CHECK

With school or club groups, a check-up on buddies is usual at the start and at intervals during the lesson. This is usually done on a whistle signal from the teacher or group leader. Activity does not resume until everyone has been accounted for.

When one adult has the responsibility of supervising a party of youngsters, the buddy system can be a great help. There are so many more eyes alert to forestall trouble.

For an intimate family group by the sea, or on the river, pairing-off into couples who can be trusted to help each other in emergencies, or better still, who can prevent accidents, should be standard procedure.

How often do you see it done? And I wonder why folk don't bother to do it? Age is no get-out. Accidents can happen to young and old alike.

Being with a partner at the swimming pool, lake or sea-side can lessen the danger, and what is more, can guarantee that help is alerted if an accident happens. My advice is:

GET THE BUDDY HABIT

CHAPTER FIFTEEN

Drownproofing the Easy Way

(P.F.)

FIG. 27. *Using the water to relax and rest.*
Taking a breath with minimum effort

UNDERSTANDING WHAT IT IS

The first and only skill of vital importance for survival is to remain at the surface comfortably for an indefinite length of time by calm, self-determined effort with minimum energy expenditure. Basically, this is drownproofing.

Swimming is a devised method of getting from here to there in water, while the strength and energy lasts, with the emphasis today all too often on speed. But it doesn't have to be.

Drownproofing is designed to keep you alive in deep water, with a minimum of movement, indefinitely. This doesn't mean swimming around in ever-decreasing circles until finally dragged under by a combination of cold, fatigue and water-logged clothing. Personal survival in deep water requires conservation of energy; swimming about or treading water won't achieve this.

In this section, we are thinking purely in terms of drownproofing, not of swimming, treading water, floating on the back, towing anyone or performing swimming tests or tricks.

SOME MORE FACTS AND DIFFERENCES

In many swimming instructional programmes, the required beginner's test is to swim one length, often with a floundering, thrashing over-arm stroke. But such a performer is about as drownproofed as a bag of cement. The attitude is wrong, because it is based upon *fighting* the water as an alien environment.

Drownproofers learn to embrace the water, to feel relaxed and at home in or under it and to enjoy the experience, not to fight it. Their achievement is based upon time spent unaided and calm in deep water, not in distance travelled at speed or in strength available before collapse.

So we see, right now, at this moment, we are not concerned with teaching a person to swim; that is a different activity and should not be confused with drownproofing.

Drownproofing is learnt by mastering a set of simple, basic water skills in a certain order, building-up to complete confidence and water-safety, by the beginner's own voluntary efforts, preferably with a buddy.

It is not achieved by a well-meaning parent dangling the child in the water and urging it to 'swim' or kick or whatever, or by supporting the child. Sorry if this seems contradictory to some of our earlier teaching efforts; but they were mainly for babies and infants, and children of that age are too young to be taught drownproofing. We are concerned now with children and adults who can understand the principle of drownproofing, and who are capable of interpreting our verbal instructions with a partner. You will have to decide at what age the child is capable of understanding what you are talking about and showing him.

MAKING A START

The true success of the exercise is dependent upon the 'sinker' discovering for himself the natural buoyancy and unsinkability of his body, with the adult out of the way. Although as we know, supervision is never relaxed.

The quickest way to drownproof your child is to take him to a professional in whom you both have confidence; reassure him you have no intention of interfering, then get out of his way.

Failing to find a professional who teaches drownproofing as distinct from swimming, then use the following set of instructions to do it yourself.

FLOATER OR SINKER?

First, establish the ability to float (breath held):

A. Waist-deep

(1) Jelly-fish float (standard). Ten per cent sinkers.

(2) Turtle-float (trunk horizontal, legs hanging, arms extended forward loosely).

B. Beyond head-depth

(3) Basic vertical float (using pool side with one-hand support).

If subject fails to float then, he is positively a sinker, and so will need to use a little more effort to stay afloat. But with 90 to 98 per cent of beginners, it can be demonstrated that they can stay at the surface with no effort beyond taking a lungful of air and holding it, *with no other movement*. This is a *vital first step*.

1. *What causes sinking?* Bone and muscle (fat floats), and the weight of the head (15 lbs) above water; or arms and hands as in waving or struggling.

2. *First principle:* keep as much of the body *below water* as

possible, most of the time, while permitting a relaxed breathing technique. It can be as simple as that.

FACE DOWN AND RELAX

When I demonstrate drownproofing, the first reaction often is, 'Oh, but you keep your face in the water. I don't think I'd like that.' Girls are too often big babies here—or are they more concerned with the preservation of make-up? Sorry!

If putting the face under water is your child's biggest bogey, then have him start practising in a basin of warm water at home, until he can keep his face submerged with eyes open, relaxed and liking it.

He'll never be drownproofed until he can master this first basic skill—common, in fact, to all swimming techniques and water sport.

Treading water isn't drownproofing yourself. The head weighs about 15 lb. Ask a person to hold a 15 lb. weight above his head while treading water, and he'll soon tire and submerge—involuntarily. Yet this, in effect, is what he tries to do with conventional stay-afloat techniques.

Floating on the back is impractical: vision is restricted to the sky, so you can't see where you're heading or what's coming, and wave-slap sends water downhill through nostrils and mouth. It is also quite difficult for those who seem unable to master the balancing knack of the horizontal float.

Take a tip from the turtle—hence my 'turtle float' for the start of drownproofing. Why fight to keep the head above water? Why not use the natural buoyancy and uplift that the combination of your body and the water can provide?

Be realistic; drop that head down, plunk! Relax and stop struggling. The hippo, alligator and seal do so with no distress. Copy them.

UNSINKABLE—HOW?

With your built-in buoyancy tanks—the lungs—and only a normal breath, the body will float steadily to the surface without any movement, no matter what its position, even if it dropped into deep water and sank initially like a stone. It would come up and stay up, if it adopted the turtle float immediately.

This re-emergence takes a surprisingly short time, if you stay calm, relaxed and motionless—and believe it will happen. But try to remember to take that normal inward breath before hitting the surface on the way into the water.

You've done it. Now you're on your way up. You are keeping loose and calm. You've got faith. Your skin is watertight and your lips are lightly pressed together to avoid scuttling. Your eyes are open so you can judge the nearness of the surface by the light-change.

Now you have reached the surface; your shoulders and back of the head are showing, face still under between the relaxed, bent arms. You stay this way, bobbing in the swell. Unbelievable maybe, but true.

'Fine, but I don't have gills. I've got to breathe.' All right. Without panic you prepare to breathe. Commence the breathing action before you actually feel the need to do so—before that panic-feeling overwhelms you. This avoids the build-up of tension and prevents the panic. Here's how:

With lips closed, still face-down, exhale through the nostrils, quite forcibly into the water. Now begin lifting the head upwards and backwards, making a gentle downward stroking movement with both palms, just a slight stroke, using forearms too if necessary.

By the time the exhalation is complete, your face should have broken the surface unhurriedly, easily, like a seal, with your mouth about an inch above the water. Inhale through the mouth and drop the face back into the water again.

If you find that you submerge a little deeper by lifting the head—nothing to be alarmed about, it's because you raised your head too high, a common fault at first; the weight of it pushed you under. This emphasises the need to keep every part of your body low in the water. Think of *using* the water, not *fighting* it.

SECONDARY STROKE

If this extra little submergence bothers you, to resume the

turtle float just make a secondary slight downward stroke with the wrists and palms before placing them loosely in front of the dropped head in the face-down resting position. You'll soon learn to move the palms like flippers and not use a big, forceful, panic-motivated stroke. Remember, you're conserving energy.

Train to maintain this resting position comfortably for 10 seconds, before starting the whole cycle over again. Now you have done it all. There is just the rhythm and timing to perfect, and you'll be drownproofed. Disappointed there's not more to it?

This is an easy action that can be performed indefinitely, becoming progressively easier and less troublesome and less tiring the longer you keep it up. It can become self-hypnotic.

Muscular activity requires oxygen. This is why treading water or swimming around for survival is tiring and impractical for drownproofing.

But the lazily resting body in the drownproofed position requires less and less oxygen, particularly if you conquer all fear and alarm, so removing the inner residual tension which is an oxygen-burner. You are hardly using the limbs, so they also do not tire. It is most restful. Eyes should remain open at all times so you can retain control, balance, judge depth, surface and so on. Sounds too easy to be true, doesn't it? Try it and see. Then teach it. Or ask your children's schools if they are teaching it— if you care enough to ask this sort of question (even if some headmasters think they're an impertinence).

COMPULSORY

Drownproofing should be introduced into all swimming programmes and *made compulsory before any swimming stroke is attempted*. Splashing and floundering across one width of the pool with held breath and screwed-up eyes is no proof that a pupil is drownproofed, or that he or she has been taught survival and water-safety.

This may upset the swimming purists and enthusiasts who only see potential champions in the pool, or the water-side squatters who prefer to gossip to a companion than get down to the responsible and strenuous task of practical teaching. But drownproofing turns a vast number of sinkers and timid toe-dabblers into confident seals and turtles, loving it.

Stroke perfection can always follow once a child, of any age, can be literally thrown into the deep end, there to bob gently, calmly, indefinitely, fully-conscious, comfortable, and safe.

ACCEPTANCE

Educational authorities in Britain differ a lot in their acceptance of the drownproofing technique and many ignore it entirely. Strange this, because wherever I've demonstrated it—schools and clubs mostly, once or twice in the sea for T.V.—enthusiasm for it has caught on fast. It can't be just anti-Americanism, can it? Ah well...

FULLY CLOTHED

Many books and authorities give much prominence to 'undressing in the water' as an essential part of survival. Well, I'm going to be awkward again and ask why?

There is the survival techniques of using clothing as impromptu buoyancy aids; removing shirt and slacks, knotting the sleeves or bottoms and blowing into them to make these floatation devices. They work fine too. But I can't imagine a sinker, or a beginner for that matter, having the presence of mind to stay calmly at the surface long enough to perform these tricks, can you?

Don't forget, we are only catering for beginners here. I'll admit, these personal survival practices are great fun with boys and girls once they have learnt to stay afloat and swim; but that's another thing. We haven't got as far as 'Survival Swimming' yet.

Here are some sound reasons for keeping your clothes on if you accidentally fall into deep water.

(a) Clothing, including footwear, will not drag you under if you can do drownproofing in salt water. Clothing *underwater* does not out-weigh the body's natural upward buoyancy, the ratio being approximately a half to one pound clothing weight to six pounds buoyancy—*underwater*.

(b) Clothing acts as insulation against cold water. The layer of water trapped next to the skin gets warmed by the body and can help the person survive in cold water twice as long as a naked body.

(c) In view of these two chief reasons, it is more practical for a beginner who has learnt drownproofing to keep his clothes on and relax, instead of struggling in a panic to rip them off.

(d) In fresh water, however, heavy top clothes like an overcoat and footwear would be best discarded, while the remaining clothing can be left on.

Four important points to remember:

1. Wet clothing weighs heavy *out of water*, so keep all clothed parts of your body underwater if you want to stay afloat. (We know about keeping the head in water as much as possible.)

2. Wet clothing creates an exhausting drag on limb action, so make slow, relaxed movements to conserve vital energy.

3. Take deeper breaths to increase internal buoyancy to counteract additional weight of clothing.

4. Be more conscious of relaxing and resting between breaths to conserve energy.

WARNING

These comments apply to persons who can do drownproofing, not to non-swimmers who cannot. It is extremely doubtful that a sinker would have the presence of mind or ability to benefit from this advice.

I know it's obvious, but it has to be faced. If a person is a helpless sinker, his only hope is to be seen and rescued quickly, or catch hold of a convenient floating object. Isn't this precisely why *we want everyone to be drownproofed*?

THEN THEY WON'T BE SINKERS—EVEN IF THEY CAN'T SWIM!

Special note: most medical authorities recommend that children with nasal or asthmatic ailments should not be compelled to learn drownproofing—or presumably any form of water activity where their faces go underwater.

Well, I'm not going to fight the medical profession right now; but to keep an asthmatic child out of water for fear of him putting his face under it, is tough on that child—in the long run.

Nasal congestion undoubtedly can cause discomfort, even panic in situations requiring large intakes of air on demand—swimming, drownproofing?

Many schoolchildren are excused running and ball games for this reason (or excuse themselves!). Consequently, they are denied the very health-giving activity that could well improve their condition.

This is an even stronger case for teaching *relaxation in water*, face out *or in*. Think about it. Try something, but with greater care and attention.

SUMMING-UP

(a) Keep eyes open at all times.

(b) Inhale before hitting the surface on the way in.

(c) Relax limbs and face, under water.

(d) Adopt the 'Turtle Float' position immediately as you rise.

(e) Exhale through nostrils forcibly prior to lifting head.

(f) Small flipper-stroke with wrists and palms downward as you lift head to clear mouth just above water-line.

(g) Inhale through mouth.

(h) Drop head down between arms which are bent at the elbows, hands loosely touching on surface.

(i) Make secondary small stroke if necessary to prevent submerging too deep after lifting head to inhale.

(j) Try to hold breath easily for 10 secs. before raising head to inhale again; but, always start breathing movement *before* you really feel the need to; this avoids tension.

(k) Tight feeling in chest? Due either to resting and holding breath too long, or exhaling too little.

(l) Shoulders must be under water and chin touching the water during the inhale—*never higher*, or you'll submerge too far.

(m) The higher the head is raised, the deeper the submergence.

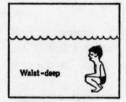

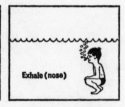

1. *Wet All Over*:
Take a breath,
duck right under,
lips and eyes shut.
Passed when im-
mersed 10 sec.
Start in bath tub.

2. *Open Eyes*:
Take a breath,
duck under; hold
breath, open eyes
wide. Count Part-
ner's fingers to
prove test. Passed 5
out of 5 correct.

3. *Blow Bubbles*:
Big breath, duck
under, lips shut,
eyes open. Exhale
through nose only.
Practise in wash-
basin.
Passed 10 out of 10
correct.

4. *Bobbing and Breathing*: Inhale above surface through
mouth, bob under, hold breath
10 sec., exhale through nose.
Rise to surface and inhale.
Repeat rhythmically. Passed
when 10 correct.

5. *Turtle Float*: Inhale with
chin on surface. Drop head,
arms loosely forward. Bend
knees, allow feet to leave
bottom. Passed with 10 sec.
float.

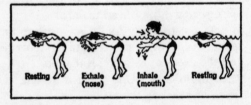

6. *Drownproofing*: First practice test: 3 min.
Passed 5 min. Passed safe: 15 mins.

FIG. 28. *Drownproofing (a brief pictorial description)*

(n) Drownproofing *is not learnt* by dangling the child in the water and urging it to 'swim' or 'kick', or by supporting it.

(o) The success of the exercise depends upon the 'sinker' discovering the natural buoyancy of his body *himself*—with non-interference from the adult.

(p) The quickest way to drownproof your child is to take him to a professional in whom you have confidence, then *get out of his way*.

(q) Failing to find a professional who teaches 'drownproofing', as distinct from swimming, then use these instructions to turn your child from a 'sinker' into a 'minnow'. Good luck!

N.B. Illustrations by courtesy of *Health For All* magazine, from the author's article 'Is Your Child Drownproofed?' of April 1968.

PART FOUR

Sinkers and Beginners at School

As a parent, or an individual non-swimmer, you may decide to give this a miss if you're not particularly interested now. But you'll want to know what should be done at school, sooner or later. As a teacher, you may be curious!

CHAPTER SIXTEEN

School's the Place

A NECESSARY REGULATION

Swimming and water-safety are not necessarily synonymous; but they should go hand-in-hand. One should be pointless without the other in a person's mind. Both should come easily, naturally to the normal child from an early age.

A boy or girl should not leave school as a qualified senior without having passed satisfactory standards in both, as judged by a recognised, national swimming and water-safety authority.

This would be one parental anxiety (and possibly responsibility) that education could relieve.

This may be an obvious statement to some people. To others, such a requirement might seem to be a violation of educational democracy—or impossibly idealistic. It depends upon upbringing and educational and political influences. But in this case, where a child's (or an adult's) ability to survive unaided in deep water is at stake, I honestly don't see how it can be left merely to chance. There must be some element of compulsion to produce the end-product of a drownproofed child while still at school.

This is where *the necessary regulation needs to be written into the educational curriculum*. On an island community like Great Britain, for example, the personal ability to survive fully clothed, in out-of-depth water from a swimming or boating accident, should be an essential and natural requirement for everyone of any age. This is not meant to over-ride personal preferences, but simply to encourage the application of commonsense. Personal survival by the learning of water-safety techniques, *as a normal and essential part of the educational process*.

GIVE IT PRIORITY

Easy-to-teach, easy-to-learn essentials for the drownproofing of children of any age, but preferably at the *primary school* level, should be top priority for all schools' physical education programmes.

The clear, straight-forward objective is to change young children from hazardous sinkers into competent swimmers, with a naturally developed love of water and the ability to enjoy it.

This is the Education Department's responsibility.

Pre-schoolers are the responsibility of parents, who should be thoroughly conversant with ways and means of waterproofing babies and young children. We have dealt with some aspects of this in Part Two and Three.

FIRST THINGS FIRST

Note I stress *competent*, not competitive or racing swimmers. Speed swimming can be introduced (in fact it's never far away) and coached to those who reveal a flair and a compulsive desire for it; but only when the child is drownproofed, safe in and around water, and has a positive urge to race.

I know many teachers of swimming claim that the most effective way of persuading children to apply themselves to pool practice, is to introduce the competitive element. 'Soon as they can get their feet off the bottom, let them race each other across the pool. They've got to have this encouragement to practise, or they'll quickly get bored and won't listen or learn.'

Yes, it's a good theory, and it may work sometimes. Just like games for example. 'They must be allowed to play and score goals early in their training, else what's the point? It can't be just skills practice all the time. Scoring goals is the whole point of the exercise. You have to teach them through fun.' And so on. But wait a bit.

Is this 'goals are all important' thing true? Surely there is more to a game than the end-product of kicking, hitting or throwing a ball into the net? What about the sheer aesthetic pleasure of movement, inter-play and combat preceding the goal? Isn't scoring goals simply a convenient, legitimate excuse for enjoying bodily activity? And so on again...

FACING ALL TEACHERS

The point I'm trying to make is, let the beginner swimmers enjoy racing across the pool, if this is your chief fun method for attracting their attention and retaining interest. You have many supporters. I'm not saying they're right!

I know there's nowhere to go when the other side is reached fast—except come back again! Aesthetically this might seem a bit futile. And also, successful teaching and learning is not necessarily only achieved by 'doing your own thing' free practice and impromptu races, although some see this as a method to provide incentive and stimulate interest. So by all means try it; but don't let it become your master.

Then again, if you are the sort of teacher who is always on the lookout for the potential school and county champion, no doubt you'll favour getting on to the racing strokes as early in their beginner training as they are able.

Please remember, however, that while concentrating on competitive swimming, you may well be neglecting many vital aspects of fun, water-safety and personal survival. You know as well as I do, swimming periods in the school curriculum are all too few and too short. You certainly can't adequately cover every essential aspect of the subject in the pitifully small amount of time allotted.

So if it's speed you're after, and if it's speed you intend to boost as all important in the children's minds, and if you are willing to be pressurised into doing it, your priorities will be different from mine.

It's a big subject and I mustn't prolong the argument here, as this isn't a schools' textbook. Like all teachers, swimming or otherwise, we have our own strongly-held points of view. The main thing is that we shouldn't be so biased that we cannot or won't see and recognise the value in the other person's methods. Controversy should stimulate continuous research and an ever-changing, ever-improving activity or product.

SURVIVAL, NOT COMPETITION

To return to our beginning theme. Primarily, the swimming teacher's responsibility (and the parents' too, of course), is to make children water-safety conscious and personally to be able to survive in a water environment. As a vital part of this education, every child must have opportunity and instruction for floating and moving through water *fully clothed*.

If this is achieved, it increases the children's active participation in a wonderfully enjoyable, health-giving sport, and widens their scope for fun and fear-free pleasure, in, on and under water, wherever they may eventually be about the world. This is providing them with the right foundation.

It will be one more immensely valuable asset to emerge from education, and so beautifully functional. The main problem: who is to provide this specialised teaching?

RESPONSIBILITY WITH THE SCHOOLS

It has to be this way, simply because all parents may not have the knowledge, ability, or even the compulsive sense of duty to teach their children about water-safety. What parents are capable of teaching elementary floating, swimming and water-survival techniques? There is no doubt, however, that all parents would want the reassurance of having their children acquire this special survival ability, so that at least their own fears may be eased!

So let us say that we hope our children will learn all about it at school, preferably primary school, better still at the infant level; but this requires enough specially designed learner pools about the country, and sympathetic, expert teachers to use them effectively. We haven't achieved this standard yet.

PARENTS MUST PLAY THEIR PART

So, therefore, anything we can do as parents to introduce the child during its infancy, or preferably babyhood, to total bodily immersion in water, with the object of water-proofing it (as against merely bathing it), should be an essential and inescapable duty. It can also be the source of great pleasure.

We need to develop within the young child, a mental condition that accepts environmental water as a completely natural part of its life, as it does the earth, country landscape and urban jungle.

The child then quickly learns to use this water as easily and effectively as it uses playground, park, or city street, with an instinctive and relaxed sense of mastery.

Can we set to and do this for our children?

CHAPTER SEVENTEEN

Ideas for School or Club Programme

ALLOW FOR INDIVIDUALITY

These are essentially ideas or suggestions, which emerged from experimentation and experience with small learner groups of young children, organised and taught in private pools of families along the west coast of British Columbia, during the long, warm, summer school vacation.

Schools generally have their own set methods of swimming instruction, and work to an established syllabus. This usually emerges from one of the national swimming and life-saving organisations, or perhaps directly from the local educational authority.

There are procedures to adopt, teach and test. Standards to achieve and reward. Some teachers may protest that there just isn't room for any more 'theories', or deviations from their normal programme—which is tight enough as it is.

They have my sympathy; I've been through the same educational mill. Yet where swimming is concerned, children are so vastly different from each other, physically, mentally and emotionally, even within the same age group, that success is not achieved by trying to force them all through some kind of educational 'mincing machine', regardless of their varying abilities. There must be allowances for individuality.

So this is where personal assessment, experimentation, exploration, and an unbiased, flexible approach is so useful and often successful with these highly individual youngsters.

Fresh, maybe novel ideas, may catch-on and work successfully with many of the hitherto 'difficult' children—where the 'set syllabus' failed. They are well worth a try, anyway, particularly as the final objective is basically the same—a *majority of children, at every age level, who can float, swim, have fun free from fear, and be safe in and around water.* And then of course, there is the wonderful health-giving fitness-forming benefit that goes with swimming.

EDUCATION NOT COMPETITION

To re-emphasise: *we should not be dominated by pressure from without, or urges from within, to make speed swimming and competition our chief motivation and preoccupation, at this sinker-learner stage.*

As educators, we cannot be happy neglecting a majority of uncertain, possible nervous beginners, for a confident, naturally talented minority—the ones who always win the races. This isn't how we interpret the objective of education, in any subject, is it?

Speed swimming and specialised competitive training is for the school club or private swimming club to develop. It shouldn't be allowed to dominate the normal, nine-to-four, educational lessons. If you are a cup-and-trophy man, then again, our priorities differ.

There is an increasing tendency to organise primary school children into competitive swimming galas. They are expected to perform correct strokes (front and back crawl, butterfly, etc.) and the racing turns.

Swimming is the youngest sport, with Olympic swimmers in their early teens, 'burnt-out' before they are twenty. A trend that causes many teachers, coaches and parents serious concern, even alarm.

But who insists on these junior swimming galas? Who is influencing the swimming teaching syllabus of schools? Are the clubs to blame? Clubs are getting younger children to join and perform (late evening sessions till 9 p.m.) when Primary School children should be in bed.

Who is changing the emphasis in school instruction from 'fun, health and safety', to competition and 'trophy glory'?

Fortunately, we can avoid alarm in our approach here, as we are concerned with the experiences of the *non-swimmers*. We want these experiences to be relaxed, enjoyable and repeatable.

So now we come back to these sinker-beginner teaching ideas. Something like them, with variations, are already being used with success in many schools. They certainly need not detract from existing instruction, but are intended to compliment and assist the learner-process.

CHAPTER EIGHTEEN

A Progressive Teaching Outline

1. *Acclimatisation and water confidence:* pupil is given time, encouragement, personalised help, the most suitable water depth (2ft 6in) and temperature (90°F) with water-safety factors observed, to become introduced to and get used to water for swimming and water play.
SUBMERGE—HOLD BREATH—OPEN EYES—EXHALE.

2. *Buoyancy (A):* pupil discovers his own buoyancy awareness through several play activities, preferably without aids.
'CROCODILES' — JELLY-FISH FLOAT — TURTLE-FLOAT — BACK-FLOAT — FRONT-FLOAT.

Buoyancy (B): approved buoyancy aids can be used initially to encourage confidence.
ARM FLOATS—SWIM-FLOAT (kick-board.).

3. *Water Entry:* pupil practises methods of *his own choice* for entering the water, progressively. WADING—SLIDING-JUMP—'STRIDE JUMP'—PLUNGE—SHALLOW DIVE.

4. *Gliding (A):* free, unaided; the start of forward movement at the surface. Initially from standing in the water once floating is achieved.
FRONT GLIDE (face down, arms stretched forward)—
BACK GLIDE (face upwards, arms streamlined at sides)—
FRONT GLIDE ROLL-OVER, STAND-UP—BACK GLIDE ROLL-OVER, STAND UP.

Gliding (B): swim-float permitted initially to help 'difficult' glider. FRONT GLIDE (float pushed ahead)—BACK GLIDE (float held over lower belly and thighs).

5. *Propulsion (A):* using swim-float—as in Gliding (B)—for front and back glide plus easy, rhythmical leg-kick. FLUTTER-KICK—FROG-KICK.

Propulsion (B): unaided; from front glide, arms only initially to concentrate on their propulsive action.
'DOG-PADDLE'—BREAST-STROKE—OVER-ARM CRAWL.

Propulsion (C): unaided; from back glide, hands and arms only. FINNING—SCULLING—ELEMENTARY BACKSTROKE.

Propulsion (D): including leg action with these strokes, once the emphasis on *arms only* has produced correct style. 'DOG-PADDLE' (flutter-kick)—BREASTSTROKE (frog-kick)—OVER-ARM CRAWL (flutter-kick)—ELEMENTARY BACKSTROKE (frog-kick with glide).

6. *Surface diving:* through play activity (picking up objects, handstand on bottom, diving through partner's legs, etc.) initially, to familiarise pupil with underwater experience and improve breath-control and general orientation.

7. *Underwater swimming:* easy, relaxed propulsion, emphasis on streamlining recovery strokes. ALTERNATE ARM ACTION (reaching and pulling) with FLUTTER-KICK—BREAST-STROKE with FROG-KICK and gliding pause.

8. *Turning and changing direction:* performed after pupil is able to swim pool width, return to starting point without touching bottom. Experiment with different methods.

9. *Swimming distance:* to build up stamina, to provide incentive and a progressive objective, to develop ability to swim strongly enough to be safe in deep water and improve water-safety. ONE WIDTH—TWO WIDTHS—FOUR WIDTHS—ONE LENGTH (start deep end)—TWO LENGTHS (start shallow end)—CONTINUOUS SWIMMING (ultimate).

10. *Jump and tread water:* teaching the pupil to have confidence in his ability to re-emerge at the surface—and stay there after jumping-in from the pool side. JUMP-ENTRY—RE-EMERGE—TREAD WATER.

11. *Drownproofing:* ability to stay at the surface with the minimum of effort for the maximum time. A personal water safety technique.

12. *Breath-control:* breathe out through nose and mouth under-

water once the beginner has started swimming-type movements. This is to ensure maximum exhalation of carbon-dioxide from the lungs without strain, and a sufficient intake of oxygen through the mouth, to supply the body's requirements increased by swimming.

NOTE: (1) Get pupils into *horizontal* position in water as soon as possible.

(2) Establish 'Buddy System' early for additional safety and mutual help and encouragement.

(3) Use of buoyancy aids should be optional. Encourage natural, unaided floating and gliding first, bringing in floats where necessary.

(4) Make the lightweight reaching pole part of the teaching procedure; use it frequently for communicating by taps on the pupil's body; as an aid for encouraging him to float, glide, do the flutter-kick; to help him enter the water; and of course, to provide something for him to hold on to should he feel nervous or wish to come out in a hurry.

(5) When teaching propulsion, emphasise *arm action only* first to develop correct style and to avoid detrimental effect (drag) of faulty leg action.

(6) Don't attempt to teach the various arm actions as separate, isolated exercises. Indicate what you want, then encourage pupils to try it out. Refinement of strokes comes later in individual coaching.

(7) In swimming for distance, pupil *competes with himself*, not with classmates. Early class competition can be destructive.

(8) Time should be allowed in each lesson for distance swimming practice.

(9) Treading water is the standard method of staying at the surface, but can be tiring for a prolonged period (boating accident in deep water), and therefore inefficient.

(10) Drownproofing left until last because this technique requires more self-confidence and self-control (economical movement and breathing) than the more conventional treading-water. A beginner should be ready for this by the time he has worked through the preceding programme.

CHAPTER NINETEEN

First Year Swimming Programme

Work through these sections and activities, encouraging pupils to master each one—with a partner or 'buddy'. Have pupils compile their own notebook list, and check-off each item as they succeed. (Detailed teaching procedure for the activities is not repeated in this chapter.)

TEACHING AND SAFETY AIDS

1. Arm-floats: one pair per child.
2. Swim-floats: one each.
3. Reaching pole.
4. Basketball timer. (A large wall clock with sweep second hand should be standard pool equipment.)
5. Nylon rope with attached floats.
6. Light ring-buoy and heaving-line.

FOR SINKERS

1. Wet all over (head must go under water).
2. Open eyes under water (buddy checks by extended fingers to be counted).
3. Blow out under water (make bubbles). *Exhale through mouth and nostrils.*
4. Bobbing and breathing 6 times. Emphasise breath-control.

FOR FLOATERS

1. Jelly-fish Float (5 secs.): partner taps floater's back when time is up.
2. Turtle Float (10 secs.): leading up to 'Drownproofing'.

3. Back Float (10 secs.): relax neck, lay head on water; make a 'big tummy'. Use side of pool with one hand to start, or kick-board.

4. Jump in from side into chest deep water (no holding). 'Stride Jump' keeping head above surface.

FOR GLIDERS
1. Front Glide (10ft) towards partner or pool side.
2. Back Glide with leg-kick (push-off from pool side).

FOR MINNOWS
1. Front Glide (5ft), raise head to 'Dog-Paddle' (5ft).
2. Back Glide with kick and 'Sculling' with hands near sides (10ft). Practise both 'Flutter-kick' and 'Frog-kick'.

FOR TROUT
1. Shallow 'dive' or plunge from steps or pool side and glide.
2. Glide and 'Dog-Paddle' (20ft).
3. Front Glide (10ft), roll over, float on back then scull (10ft).
4. Tread water 30 secs. (shoulder deep).
5. 'Dog-Paddle' (10ft). Convert it to beginning 'Sidestroke' with one cheek on water (20ft).
6. Back Glide from push-off, scull (10ft), change to 'Elementary Back Stroke' with 'Frog-kick' (10ft). Aim for total pool width.
7. Jump entry, tread water for one minute (just out of depth). Practise both 'Stride Jump' and 'Vertical Jump'.

FOR SHARK
1. Surface dive to pick-up object from pool bottom.
2. Surface dive and underwater swim (10ft initially; aim for 20ft).
3. Distance swimming (pool width—two widths—one length).
4. Drownproofing (1. waist-deep; 2. just out of depth). First test 3 mins. Passed safe 15 mins.

SINKERS AND BEGINNERS: LESSON IDEA A

First 5 mins. Wet all over. 'Bouncing Balls' (aim for greatest height, deepest depth); 'Coupled Tag'.

Second 5 mins. 'Show me what you can do, or have learnt.' 'Bobbing and Blowing' (gulp air in above surface, bob under and blow out through mouth and nostrils).

Third 5 mins. 'Jelly-fish Float'; 'Torpedoes' with kick-boards; 'Turtle Float'; Front Glide and stand up; Front Glide—beginning 'Dog-Paddle'.

Fourth 5 mins. Free play and individual practice. (Teacher alert to assist with instruction any pupil who seems to need it or asks for it.)

Suggestion: avoid regimentation and conventional idea of 'class instruction' (militancy, taking turns, etc). Fear-free enjoyment with safety the main aim.

Gradually introduce idea and theme of 'Drownproofing' (from the 'Turtle Float').

OLDER PUPILS: LESSON IDEA B

First 5 mins. Free play and/or practice: (incentive to undress quickly and get wet all over).

Second 5 mins. 'Show me and the class, your best stroke or stunt' (in fours); 'Line Tag' by teams (escape by diving under and through arches).

Third 5 mins. ('Swimmers' at deeper end doing training/ practice; remainder doing widths—'Torpedoes' with or without kick-boards; 'Front Glide' with leg-beat; 'Front Crawl' stroked without and with breathing; breathing techniques holding side rail; 'Turtle Float' leading to 'Drownproofing'.

Fourth 5 mins. Free practice: individual instruction or coaching; teacher moving about freely, encouraging and praising.

Suggestion: Try 'Buddy System' ('Find your buddy'). Practices with buddy (leading to lifesaving). Plastic lightweight ball(s) for play, floating aid and for water sport—'Polo';

'Heads-Up' (keeping ball in air greatest number of times); 'Under-and-Over-Relay'; etc.

SWIMMING AND WATER-SAFETY: SCHOOL BEGINNER'S TEST

1. Water-safety knowledge: teacher sets questions.
2. Reaching aids (3): pupil demonstrates correctly.
3. Open eyes under water: either teacher, or partner checks.
4. Bobbing and breathing six times continuously.
5. Jelly-fish float (10 secs.).
6. Turtle float (15 secs.).
7. Front glide, roll over, hold, stand up.
8. Back glide, roll over, hold, stand up.
9. Swim on front (20ft), turn about, return.
10. Sculling on back with flutter-kick (20ft), turn about, return using frog-kick.
11. 'Stride Jump' entry, keeping head above surface, tread water (30 secs.), return to side and climb out. Water above head depth.
12. Plunge entry from side, glide, 'Dog-Paddle' (with breathing) or 'Front Crawl' (with or without breathing) across pool, climb out.

N.B. These water skills and activities, and the test, can be given full publicity if the pool has a wall-side notice-board for pin-ups. Draw out charts that can be read at a distance. Alternatively, make use of chalk boards.

Teacher will modify and vary the activities and tests according to existing policy, facilities and size of classes. It is the almost 'normal' occurrence of over-large classes that so frequently upsets and prevents application of fresh ideas, and forces the teacher to use militant and dogmatic methods.

Classes of 30 to 40 children are accepted as 'normal', although educational theory stresses that these can only handicap learning and make class control difficult. Small learner-groups of from 12 to 20 are recommended. We would gladly welcome such conditions; but we all are forced to handle far larger classes as an inevitable part of our daily teach-experience. Will we ever be able to approach nearer to the educational ideal?

CHAPTER TWENTY

The Classroom Learner Pool

WHAT DOES THIS MEAN?

It means simply taking over a classroom or small hall and installing a sectional, above-ground, shallow-water 'Learner' pool from one of the specialist firms.

This was originally pioneered by the Craven Park Primary School in London in the early 1960s, was an obvious success from the start, and has never been regretted in any way since.

Mr. H. V. Howard was the progressive headmaster to introduce that project, and still is—energy and enthusiasm unimpaired, as buoyant as ever. Perhaps the only critical comment we can make is that he is a dedicated man in this field—sorry, pool!

Dedication is not a commonplace trait. Trouble is, it frequently requires you to think more of your job than of yourself. A difficult quality to match sometimes. But I'm not selling Harold Howard, just cashing-in on his ideas about teaching beginners to swim—in a classroom!

MORE TO THE POINT

This is what it is, basically. (Then I'll tell you what it does, and leave it up to you.)

(a) *Classroom 'Learner' Pool:* strong, permanent construction of specially treated timber cavity walls, steel reinforced and lined with heavy gauge vinyl, supplied in sections for easy handling and erection. (Materials and construction vary with different firms, but the effect is more or less the same.)

(b) *Water depth:* A 3ft model is recommended for instructional purposes, where the depth of water can be reduced to as little as 16in to 18in for the shallow-water method. On the other hand, a depth of 30in to 32in is suitable for adult swimming instruction.

An example of specifications
(Purley 'Olympic' model)

	Outside dias. (feet)	Capacity (galls)	Surface area (sq. ft)	Max. No. recommended for instr. (children)		
				One per 24 sq. ft	One per 4ft rail or rope	Number of children
1	17 × 9 × 3	2,000	128	5	4	4
2	25 × 9 × 3	3,000	192	8	6	7
3	25 × 17 × 3	6,000	384	16	12	14
4	33 × 17 × 3	8,000	512	21	16	18
5	41 × 17 × 3	10,000	640	26	20	23
6	49 × 17 × 3	12,000	768	32	24	28
7	33 × 25 × 3	12,000	768	32	20	26
8	41 × 25 × 3	15,000	960	40	24	32
9	49 × 25 × 3	18,000	1152	48	28	38

(c) *Learner rails:* white plastic-coated steel. Double rails are best for the shallow pool where the water-level can be reduced: one at water level, one eight inches lower.

The feet can be supported by the lower rail with the hands on the pool bottom (or on a float); or the other way around with the hands on the rail. Kicking, breathing, arm-action can be practised and coached this way.

(d) *Equipment:* steps, heaters, filtration plant, chemical kits, swim-floats ... have to be considered for a complete instructional pool, but this is normal expenditure.

(e) *Further facts:* naturally, you will need to know many more facts about this type of pool. These can all be supplied by the different firms when you make your enquiries and ask for details of construction and use. You will recall the four firms I mentioned earlier in Chapter One.

(f) *Cost:* prices increase, year-by-year, as with everything; but nevertheless, the cost of installing this sort of fully-equipped pool was equivalent to equipping a classroom with furniture and fittings, with a running cost of around £5 ($13) a week.

By using off-peak current, giving a temperature of 90°F in the morning, dropping to 86°F by 4.30 p.m., the cost could be reduced, but still maintaining enjoyable, comfortable water for instruction. Ideal temperatures in fact.

Put another way: it is cheaper and more practical in every way for a school to have its own classroom pool, than to take its pupils by coach to the public baths.

WHAT THIS POOL CAN DO

(a) For a start, it permits and encourages effective, enjoyable, safe teaching for nearly 100% of pupils a minimum of two half-hour sessions each week. Public pools are generally overbooked by schools and classes who do not have enough actual water time to enjoy effective teaching. Most classes spend more time in the bus than in the water. Why should this be tolerated as normal or inevitable? Re-thinking at City/County Hall!

(b) The classroom pool becomes an outstanding educational influence. It encourages a more relaxed and effective teacher-pupil relationship, where children approach the headmaster with more ease and confidence than they do their own fathers. (That is, if the head participates.)

(c) Specialist swimming teachers are not required. A child should have great confidence in his own class teacher. This teacher should know his pupils intimately and get good results because of it, even though he may be a poor swimmer himself.

(d) With this type of structure, the teacher is on the same working level as his pupils, a great physical and psychological advantage.

(e) It turns out swimmers at literally an amazing rate, with every child a swimmer and 'drownproofed' by the age of nine or younger.

Introduction of stroke technique in the learner pool instead of at the public baths caused an immediate and startling improvement and increase.

In this primary school, the swimming and water-safety programme, conducted on a friendly, personal basis, exerted a positive influence on all the children from their entry in the first year and upwards.

CRAVEN PARK PRIMARY SCHOOL, LONDON
PROGRESSIVE ACHIEVEMENT WITH THE PURLEY CLASSROOM POOL

YEAR	WATERBORNE	50 YARDS	100 YARDS
1960	32%	16%	14%
1961	93%	57%	43%
1962	98%	60%	45%
1963	98%	83%	82%
1964	98%	83%	81%
1965	98%	90%	90%
1966	100%	100%	100%

It improved their social behaviour and increased their confidence in other subjects. The staff are emphatic: the tone and efficiency of the whole school has greatly improved since their classroom pool was installed. It is not just a pool, but an educational aid which pays for itself over and over again.

Final comment from Harold Howard, headmaster: 'The gimmick angle of this pool ended within six months. Now I believe it to be the complete answer to swimming and water-safety for young children (including the very young) as well as adults.'

To support this: there is a waiting list of adults to take lessons, and all the members say the shallow depth and warmth are the pool's greatest assets. As the head so aptly states:

'IT IS NEITHER NECESSARY NOR DESIRABLE TO TAKE CHILDREN TO A POOL IN WHICH THEY CAN DROWN IN ORDER TO TEACH THEM TO SWIM.'

PART FIVE

Useful Things to Know

Once you get personally involved in the water element on a friendly basis, like now, there's endless scope for fun and fitness, play-time, leisure-time, even work-time activity with great health and pleasure potential. So the more you know about it the better. That's a fact!

CHAPTER TWENTY-ONE

Personal Hygiene and Safety

This personal hygiene is a big thing in a person's life. No maybe about it. It's bigger than money and better than power. Even an animal is naturally cleaner than many humans: (have you ever known an animal with smelly feet?). And if a human doesn't pay any heed to hygiene, then he's lower than an animal —with apologies to the animal.

An animal is just naturally clean, biologically clean to function: (it's humans who make pigs, cattle and poultry dirty). A human generally needs to have a reason to be clean. And what better reason than being a swimmer? Then everyone benefits.

What I'm saying is, you've got to be clean before you hit that water. A swimming pool isn't a free wash.

Just think of all the bodies passing through a public pool in a day. How do you see yourself as part of that? Clean before you dive in—the way you hope they all are? You do think about it, don't you? So now we get down to it.

1. *Total body shower* must be mandatory. It must be as naturally habitual before entering the pool as washing the hands before a meal, or cleaning the teeth before bed.

2. There shouldn't be a swimming pool these days which permits access to the pool deck without being forced to go through a shower first. And this isn't just idealism, neither does it refer to school classes only.

3. *Running water, disinfected foot baths* have got to be an essential part of the set-up. If there's any pool where this isn't so right now, then they've got to be built-in double-quick. But surely, local councils know about things like this? Don't they?

4. *Wearing of swim-caps* by persons with long hair, male or female, should be a rule too.

5. *Spitting and spouting* of water should be forbidden.

6. *Spectators* and *anyone wearing street shoes* should be kept off the pool deck.

7. *Regular foot inspections* should be made by teachers of classes before proceeding with the lesson in the water.

8. *Chewing gum and eating sweets* shouldn't be allowed at the pool.

9. *Swimming costumes* shouldn't be thrown or kicked about the changing-rooms, and should be washed after use.

All this sort of thing is a joint responsibility of the pool management, the visiting teacher and the individual swimmer. Other personal hygiene rules are largely left to the swimmer's sense of cleanliness and conscience, such as:

10. Using lavatory facilities before swimming, whether you feel the need to or not. Certainly a good opportunity to blow the nose and clear the throat of excessive mucus. This must be done.

11. Getting the grease and guk out of your hair, and the smelly, decomposing skin between your toes cleaned-up before you go on to the pool deck.

12. Keeping away from the pool entirely if you suffer from colds, chest and throat infection, or skin complaints like *Athletes Foot*, which is very resistant. Thorough drying of the feet, especially between the toes, after swimming and showering is one of the best preventive measures. And always have a pair of rubber 'flippers' with you to reduce actual bare-foot contact in these public places.

Most infections thrive under conditions of warmth and moisture, and are more likely to be transmitted in locker-rooms and changing areas. Infectious diseases actually caused by polluted pool water are rare.

Modern pools are strictly controlled by the department of the Medical Officer for Health. Any health hazards are more likely to occur in the changing, showering and toilet areas through overcrowding, poor ventilation and neglectful personal hygiene. So this is where the individual responsibility lies.

We come back to individual health standards every time.

VERY PERSONAL

Just think about yourself a moment. When you remove your shoes and socks, are you honestly satisfied with (or indifferent to) what you see and smell? Of course, you shouldn't be able to smell anything at all. Same thing about your underwear.

Some folk are shockers with things like this. It's just as if they have a mental blockage about the state of their own bodily hygiene. They simply allow the dirt to build-up in the nooks and crannies of their bodies, while they appear to remain totally unconcerned, even when they strip-off in public. Consequently, bacteria and other micro-organisms have a birthday (or a honeymoon!), multiplying like mad in their role of decomposing the matter and enjoying a free banquet at your (and others) expense. This is where the offensive smell develops. You can't blame the bacteria!

Oh, by the way. I'm not being too personal, am I?

So what do we do about it? The answer is simple enough; but the translating of it into regular action I'm afraid requires a considerable effort on a regular day-to-day basis. It can be so easy not to do it.

GET THE DAILY, AFTER WORK SHOWER HABIT, or MORNING AND EVENING STRIPWASH, if you haven't got a shower handy, paying special attention to armpits, groin, sexual and excretory organs and feet.

Now for the Safety

ONLY OURSELVES TO BLAME

In so many ways we can be our own worst enemy and in our enjoyable water-world of swimming, boating, fishing and the like, the water isn't at fault when we suffer an accident—we are, through:

IGNORANCE, INEXPERIENCE, CARELESSNESS, NEGLECT, or even OVER-CONFIDENCE.

This is why being able to swim is vitally important for everyone, because a swimmer can have a greater chance of saving himself in a water emergency. You would think he knows what to do.

But this isn't the end of it. Ignorance and stupidity cause so many mishaps in and around water, and result in PANIC, even with some swimmers.

SWIMMERS AREN'T IMMUNE

It's always shocking to learn that a good swimmer has drowned, or has had to be rescued. It astonishes some people. They can't imagine why it happened. Perhaps what they don't realise is that even a proficient swimmer can over-reach himself; can be foolishly over-confident or neglectful, and suddenly suffer the unexpected difficulty, mishap or accident. Just as drivers on the roads do. And swimming isn't synonymous with commonsense, intelligence, or regard for others.

NON-SWIMMERS AND BEGINNERS CAN BE SAFER

Hard to believe? They can be more aware of their own short-comings and lack of ability, and so take less chances, perhaps be even more careful, cautious in and around water; but only if they have the awareness and the commonsense. This is what we're concerned with.

But hold hard! We're not making out a case for not bothering to learn swimming. There's no excuse for that. Everyone has got to have some water ability. Some time or other, most of us are going to be unexpectedly exposed to the hazards of deep water. It's inevitable.

RESPONSIBILITY OF EVERY MAN, WOMAN AND CHILD

Everyone should be able to save himself in this kind of emergency, and be capable of assisting, maybe saving his fellow man in such a situation.

Adults should give their children every opportunity to achieve this ability. It's an essential part of their role as parents and teachers.

Likewise, children must be willing to learn, practise and improve their swimming and water-safety knowledge and personal ability. None of us can escape this duty—or want to.

HOW ARE WE TO DO IT?

I could go on and reel off lists of do's and don'ts, quoting (or pirating) large chunks of existing books on the subject. Instead, I'm urging you to spend a few pence, not a lot, and get hold of this literature especially written for the non-swimmer/beginner/teaching market, with special emphasis on water-safety. You can afford it. Make the effort. You can't afford not to. Here's what I mean:

The Teaching of Swimming: issued by The Amateur Swimming Association, Acorn House, 314 Gray's Inn Road, London, W.C.1.

Get Swimming: A Sure Guide to Confidence in the Water, by H. V. Howard and D. P. Grainger. (Souvenir Press Ltd., 95 Mortimer Street, London, W.1.).

The Father and Son Swimming Book, by Howard Liss & Phillip E. Moriarty. (Pelham Books Ltd., 52 Bedford Square, London W.C.1. U.S.A.: Harper & Row, Inc., 49 East 33rd Street, New York.)

Swimming For Schools by A. H. Owen (Pelham Books Ltd.).

Life Saving and Water Safety, by The Royal Life Saving Society, 14 Devonshire Street, Portland Place, London, WIN 2 AT. 30p plus postage.

On the Water, in the Water, by The Royal Society for the Prevention of Accidents, Royal Oak Centre, Brighton Road, Purley, Surrey, CR2 2 UR. 10p post free.

Supplementary Notes to Instructor Guide and Reference, and the *Water Safety Manual,* by The Canadian Red Cross Society Water Safety Service, 95 Wellesley Street, E, Toronto, Canada.

Now there are others, obviously. But we're concerned right now with tackling the non-swimmer and beginner problem, and with promoting commonsense water-safety. This is where our energies are directed. Other books, some with international reputation, take swimming instruction too far beyond our beginner level, and would confuse the issue with us; although we do list them in our 'Further Reading' section, and respect and admire their technical and professional approach. These are the sort of books you will make good use of as soon as you have passed the beginner stage and are looking for someone to take you further.

SOME BASIC RULES FOR PERSONAL SAFETY

1. No running or horseplay on the pool deck, (including no running dives from the pool side).

2. Do not swim near or under diving boards.

3. Before diving or jumping in, make sure the area is clear of swimmers.

4. Come out of the water as soon as you feel chilly; (if your fingers and toes become numb, you've been in too long).

5. Never paddle, bathe or swim alone, or immediately after a meal.

6. Remember that floating toys, air-beds, rings and the like can be a hazard by carrying you out of your depth: (currents, tides and wind).

7. As a non-swimmer or poor swimmer, you should wear a life-jacket when boating, sailing and canoeing.

8. Beware of soft mud, quicksand and pot-holes.

9. Don't play around in rivers, streams, lakes, ponds, canals or gravel pits. You must be an experienced swimmer to use these places, and then of course, never alone.

10. Don't stand up or change places in a canoe or dinghy, it can so easily rock dangerously or even capsize.

11. If your boat or canoe capsizes, STAY WITH IT and try to attract attention.

12. Don't play around with rafts and similar floating objects, fun though it may be.

13. Avoid fishing alone, especially on weak, eroded or crumbling banks.

14. If suddenly in deep-water difficulty: keep calm (panic increases the danger), call for help, try to relax and float (on the back, or by the 'Drownproofing' method), try to attract attention by waving one arm, (two arms in the air will push you under).

15. Start learning to swim for distance as soon as you change from non-swimmer to beginner: it will build-up your strength, confidence and ability to resist fatigue.

16. Learn to swim before attempting to practise other water sports.

NOW GET THAT LITERATURE FOR ALL THE OTHER RULES YOU NEED.

CHAPTER TWENTY-TWO

Where and When to Swim

Favourite swimming places often have unexpected hazards. The worst hazard is the trick we play on ourselves: 'It can never happen to me!' Swimmers, naturally, enjoy this misconception. They certainly aren't immune to accident, although you would imagine they know enough to keep out of trouble. You'd imagine wrong.

It's easy to shrug and say 'It's only a matter of common-sense'. Trouble is, water-safety is so basically simple, that we often over-look the simplest precautions. So there are people who fail to check swimming places for safety, and then get into difficulty in the water. Folk like that are a hazard to other people as well.

WHERE TO SWIM
1. *Depth:* to a maximum of 10ft or less, with a firm, gradually sloping bottom. (Deeper water is dangerous because rescue from the bottom is difficult.)

2. In water personally recommended by a responsible person who knows it, and preferably supervised.

3. In areas marked by red and yellow flags to indicate 'Patrolled by Lifeguards'.

4. In water shallow enough to wade in from shore, and in the shallow end of the pool if only a beginner.

5. In ponds or lakes where the bottom can be seen. This means clear, unpolluted water.

6. Swim within your depth and in line with the shore or bank.

7. Swim with others, certainly with a buddy, and where adult supervision is available.

8. Above all, in well-known water, especially where the nature of the bottom is known and judged safe, and where there are no strong currents or tides.

WHERE NOT TO SWIM

1. In water of unknown depth, or in strange places.

2. In cloudy, murky, polluted water.

3. Where red flags indicate 'Dangerous to Swim' or 'Unsafe to Bathe'.

4. Don't swim out to sea, across a river, after drifting objects —or *alone* at any time.

5. In gravel pits, unless with a strong swimmer, or responsible adult supervision.

(a) The water is always deep and cold, the sides steep.

(b) They are generally private, isolated and away from the public, with little chance of cries being heard if you got into difficulty.

6. In canals, alone. Sides are steep, the water can be deep with weed-covered bottom. Very difficult to get out alone.

7. In unsupervised rivers, streams or lakes.

(a) The bottom often slopes steeply, you are quickly out of depth.

(b) Hidden objects—old tree trunks, rocks, weeds, sharp rusty metal, tin cans, broken bottles, etc. may trap or injure you.

(c) Fast currents or undertows may sweep you away.

8. Gravel pits, canals, rivers and lakes are definitely not for beginners, fun though they may be.

9. Never beyond waist-depth in the sea, or on an ebb tide near sand-spits, rocks or headlands. These are often swept by fast-moving tides.

10. In secluded spots alone.

11. Never swim out with the current—it may be impossible to return.

12. Don't paddle, wade or swim in ponds or lakes with a soft, muddy bottom. Beware of soft, sinking mud. Check first with a long stick or pole.

13. Don't dive from a boat or raft into unknown water. You never know what you may hit, or where you might end up.

14. *A repeat:* never swim alone, anywhere.

WHEN TO SWIM

1. During the warmest and most pleasant time of day: late morning, early afternoon.

2. *Before* meals. A pre-breakfast swim can be invigorating, if with a partner, or supervised. But you need to be an active *swimmer* and a special breed for this kind of exercise.

3. When you have satisfied yourself the area is safe, supervised and danger-free.

WHEN NOT TO SWIM

1. Right after a meal. Wait at least two hours after eating before going into the water. Your body needs its energy initially to digest the food, and not have it diverted to keep you warm in cold water, and to supply active muscles in swimming and water-play. To swim after a meal, is to create conflict between the digestive system and active motor muscles.

2. *Never after dark.* Supervision is impossible, and so is rescue if you go under. Boats are a hazard too—their occupants can't see in the dark!

3. When fatigued by some other sport, tired or very hot. Wait a while, cool off and recover. Then don't dive straight into cold water. Wade in and splash yourself to accustom your heated body to the drastic lowering of temperature.

4. In an overcrowded pool. Diving is certainly out.

5. When you are apprehensive and uncertain of your ability. This is when you need the reassurance and physical support of an experienced partner, parent or professional teacher.

SAFE—NOT SORRY

Then you'll be around to enjoy another day. So please don't dismiss this section as a lot of spoil-sport do's and don'ts. Dare I say it? It's for your own good! I know, most of us don't want to be done good by. But gosh! It's very handy to have a little practical know-how for the occasion. You've got to admit that. And besides, it'll increase your enjoyment. Ah, now that's something.

NOTE: We are using the term 'swim' in this context to mean any form of water bathing, paddling, swimming and general recreation of that nature.

CHAPTER TWENTY-THREE

The Kiss of Life (emergency ventilation)

This means getting enough air into a person's lungs when he is unable to breathe and do it for himself. In our case, we are concerned with giving emergency help quickly to a person who has been rescued from a water accident. It could happen to anyone. We ought to have a fair idea of what to do, even if we never have to use the knowledge. But you never can tell.

THE EXPIRED AIR METHOD

The R.L.S.S. states emphatically: '... this is the only really efficient method.' But as this is commonly known as 'the mouth-to-mouth method', (in fact, mouth-to-nose is better), it tends to put a lot of people off. Never mind, it doesn't have to any more. I'll explain the method, then give you information on a new development.

The Kiss of Life

PREPARATION

1. Vital to get oxygen (air) into the person's lungs with the *minimum* delay.

2. Check to see if breathing has stopped: look for discoloration of lips, nails, ears, cheeks, or movement of chest.

3. Put person carefully on to his back, head a bit higher than feet.

4. Tilt the head back and lift the jaw (to shift tongue away from back of throat).

(P.F.)

FIG. 29. *Tilting the head back*

5. Clear any blockage of mouth and throat.

6. Check for breathing again. If still no signs, then start the emergency ventilation immediately, keeping his head tilted back.

VENTILATION

1. Cup the patient's chin with your hand to *close his mouth*, pressing his lips together with your thumb.

2. Take a medium-full breath.

3. Place your mouth over the patient's nostrils to make a tight seal.

4. Blow gently into his nostrils and check to see if his *chest rises*. (If it doesn't, you are not making a good enough seal.)

5. Remove your mouth, turn head and inhale and check to see if *chest falls*.

6. Repeat the process, with fairly quick breaths: BLOW-IN—

REMOVE MOUTH, INHALE—BLOW-IN—REMOVE MOUTH, INHALE—and repeat about *one every second*.

7. DO NOT BLOW-IN VIOLENTLY: (the mouth-to-nose method helps to prevent any internal damage by over-inflation).

8. Repeat this in-out cycle about four or six times.

9. Slow down this cycle to about 12 times a minute (one every 5 seconds).

(a) The slower rate has a chance of matching the patient's own breathing rhythm (or stimulating his respiratory system to re-start).

(b) It prevents the operator from getting giddy through hyper-ventilation.

10. Check his chest wall for movement: if there are no signs it may be because

(a) not a good enough seal over his nose and mouth, or

(b) airways still obstructed and need clearing.

11. Patient's 'pink' colour will return to replace the 'blue' look if this emergency ventilation is successful. This is the time to stop; but continue holding his chin up to keep his throat clear.

NOTE A: to do this to a baby, make a seal with your mouth over his nose and mouth and blow-in gently by puffing your cheeks. NO HARD BLOWING. Perform a 20-25 times a minute cycle.

NOTE B: if the nose is obstructed, change to mouth-to-mouth method. Same principle, but pull lower jaw down to open mouth, and close nostrils by pinching with thumb and fore-finger.

(P.F.)

FIG. 30. *Mouth-to-nose ventilation*

PORTEX 'RESUSCIADE'*

(a) Small nylon mouthpiece with one-way valve, surrounded by a soft P.V.C. sheet, 8in × 8in.

(b) Folds up tidily into a 2in square, handy for pocket or first aid kit.

(c) Designed by a British policeman, and is particularly useful for demonstration and practice of the mouth-to-mouth method by teachers and classes.

(d) Sold direct from factory in minimum quantities of ten.

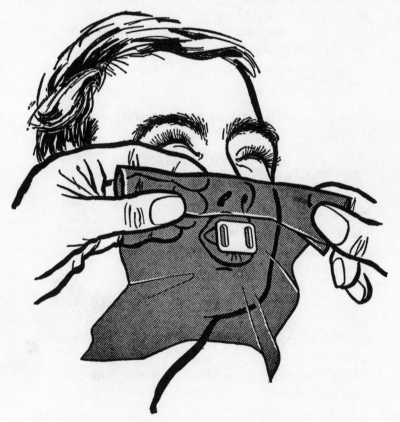

FIG. 31. *The 'Resusciade'*

* Obtainable from Portex Limited, Hythe, Kent.

(e) Especially useful for those who shy at mouth-to-mouth contact with strangers, or same sex.

(f) Also helps to prevent over-ventilation.

FINAL COMMENT

This 'Expired Air Ventilation' is the most efficient and safest method for the layman or person with little or no knowledge of other methods. In fact, they can all be quite confusing. So if we stick to this really practical method advised by the R.L.S.S., A.S.A. and others, and maybe have a 'Resusciade' handy too, we should do all right.

For more detailed information, you should study their booklets. I'm listing them.

CHAPTER TWENTY-FOUR

Useful Contacts

SWIMMING INSTRUCTION

Amateur Swimming Association:

Acorn House, 314 Gray's Inn Road, London, W.C.1.
(Telephone: 01-278 6751)

Scottish A.S.A.:
Mr. P. Boyd, 20 Farm Avenue, Porton, Lasswade, Midlothian.

Welsh A.S.A.:
Mr. W. Hooper, 45 Devon Place, Newport, Monmouthshire.

Irish A.S.A.:
Mr. D. McCullough, 11 Merok Crescent, Belfast, BT6 9LZ, Northern Ireland.

Ulster Branch A.S.A.:
Mr. J. Stevenson, 5 Hillside Drive, Belfast 9, Northern Ireland.

English Schools Swimming Association:
Mr. D. W. Morris, The School House, Windlesham, Surrey.

Useful Contacts

Swimming Teachers Association:
1 Birmingham Road, West Bromwich, Staffordshire.

British Swimming Coaches Association:
Mr. G. E. Bole, 26 Whitby Avenue, Fartown, Huddersfield, Yorkshire.

National School of Swimming:
Mr. R. H. Brickett, 11 South Lodge Drive, London, N.14.

Scottish Schools Swimming Association:
Mr. T. Ritchie, 'Tynecroft', Old Greenock Rd., Bishopton, Renfrewshire.

'Learn to Swim—Scotland' Committee:
Mr. J. B. Robb, S.C.P.R., 16 Royal Crescent, Sauchiehall Street, Glasgow, C.3.

National Association of Swimming Clubs for the Handicapped:
123 Cole Green Lane, Welwyn Garden City, Hertfordshire.

Central Council of Physical Recreation:
26-29 Park Crescent, London, W1N 4 AJ.
(Telephone: 01-580 6822/9)

British Sub-Aqua Club:
160 Gt. Portland Street, London, W1N 5TB.

SWIMMING AND WATER-SAFETY

Royal Life Saving Society:
Desborough House, 14 Devonshire Street, Portland Place, London, W.1. (Telephone: 01-580 5678/5679)

R.L.S.S. Scottish Branch:
Mr. G. J. C. Rae, 36 Bolton Drive, Mount Florida, Glasgow, S.2.

R.L.S.S. Ulster Branch:
Mrs. I. Johnson, 43 Lyndhurst Parade, Belfast, Northern Ireland.

Royal Society for the Prevention of Accidents: (RoSPA) Water Safety Service:
Royal Oak Centre, Brighton Road, Purley, Surrey, CR2 2UR.
(Telephone: 01-668 4272)

The Surf Life Saving Association of Gt. Britain:
4 Cathedral Yard, Exeter, Devon.

GENERAL

British Long Distance Swimming Association:
Mr. J. K. Slater, 29 St. Albans Avenue, Skircoat Green, Halifax.

Channel Swimming Association:
Mr. J. D. Floydd, 8 Manor Road, Folkestone, Kent.

The Scout Association:
25 Buckingham Palace Road, London, S.W.1.
(Telephone: 01-834 6005)

Girl Guides Association:
17-19 Buckingham Palace Road, London, S.W.1.
(Telephone: 01-834 6242)

National Association of Boys Clubs:
17 Bedford Square, London, W.C.1.
(Telephone: 01-636 5357)

National Association of Youth Clubs:
30-32 Devonshire Street, London, W.1.
(Telephone: 01-935 2941)

National Council of Y.M.C.A.s:
112 Great Russell Street, London, W.C.1.
(Telephone: 01-636 8954)

The Physical Education Association:
Ling House, 10 Nottingham Place, London, W1M 4AX.
(Telephone: 01-486 1301-2)

Names and addresses of many other organisations concerned with water activities are listed in the RoSPA booklet *On the Water, in the Water*, plus a complete list of the National Water Safety Committee.

AMERICAN AND CANADIAN ORGANISATIONS

American Association for Health, Physical Education and Recreation:
1201 16th Street NW, Washington, D.C. 20036, U.S.A.

American Red Cross Society, Water Safety Service:
17th Street between D & E, N.W., Washington D.C., U.S.A.

Useful Contacts

National Water Safety Congress:
Lake Cumberland Reservoir, Jamestown, Kentucky 42629, U.S.A.

College Swimming Coaches Association of America:
P.O. Box 80, New Smyrna Beach, Florida 32069, U.S.A.

National Council of Y.M.C.A.s, Health and Physical Education:
291 Broadway, New York 10007, N.Y., U.S.A.

National Council Boy Scouts of America:
New Brunswick, N.J., U.S.A.

National Executive Director, Girl Scouts of the U.S.A.:
830 Third Avenue, New York 10022, N.Y., U.S.A.

Boys' Clubs of America:
Director: 381 Fourth Avenue, New York 10016, N.Y., U.S.A.

President's Council on Youth Fitness:
441 G Street, N.W., Washington 25, D.C., U.S.A.

National Recreation Association:
8 West Eighth Street, New York 10011, N.Y., U.S.A.

National Health Council:
1790 Broadway, New York 10019, N.Y., U.S.A.

Canadian Red Cross Society, Water Safety Service:
95 Wellesley St. E., Toronto, Canada.

Canadian Association for Health, Physical Education and Recreation:
333 River Road, Vanier City, Ontario KiL 8B9., Canada.

Boys' Clubs of Canada:
National Office, 35 York Street, Montreal 215, Quebec, Canada.

Boy Scouts of Canada:
P.O. Box 5151, Postal Station F., Ottawa 5, Ontario, Canada.

Girl Guides of Canada Inc.,
50 Morton Street, Toronto 295, Canada.

National Council of Y.M.C.A.s of Canada:
National Physical Education Committee:
2160 Yonge Street, Toronto (7), Canada.

CHAPTER TWENTY-FIVE

Other Swimming Literature

BOOKS

The Teaching of Swimming: issued by The Amateur Swimming Association. (First published 1919, ninth edition 1968, reprinted 1970.)

Survival Swimming: by J. A. Holmyard. (Also published by A.S.A.)

Get Swimming: A Sure Guide to Confidence in the Water: by H. V. Howard and D. P. Grainger. (Souvenir Press Ltd., London. 1966.)

The Father and Son Swimming Book: by Howard Liss & Phillip E. Moriaty. (Pelham Books Ltd., London. U.S.A.: Harper & Row Inc.)

Swimming for Schools: by A. H. Owen. (Pelham Books Ltd., London.)

The Science of Swimming: by Dr. James Counsilman. (Pelham Books Ltd., London. U.S.A.: Prentice Hall Inc.)

Swimming: by Frank Waterman. (Teach Yourself Books. New ed. 1970.)

Swimming and Diving: by David Alvin Armbruster and others. (Kaye & Ward, London. 5th edition 1970.)

Swimming and Diving: the official coaching book of the E.S.S.A. (Heinemann. Revised edition 1969.)

Life Saving and Water Safety: by the Royal Life Saving Society.

Supplementary Notes to Instructor Guide and Reference: and the *Water Safety Manual*: by The Canadian Red Cross Society, Water Safety Service, Toronto.

YMCA Swimming Manual: by the National Physical Education Committee, National Council of Y.M.C.A.s of Canada, 2160 Yonge St., Toronto (7), Canada.

Other Swimming Literature

MAGAZINES

The Swimming Times: 10p (by post £1.50 p.a.).

The Swimming World (American): £3.53 p.a. both from A.S.A., Acorn House, 314 Gray's Inn Road, London W.C.1.

Swimming Pool Review: quarterly. 80p p.a. post free from Readers Service (SPR), Armour House, Bridge Street, Guildford, Surrey.

Last Word

I haven't handed this to you on a plate, neither have I made everything so easy there's no need for you to do any work on it, I hope. The whole idea is that you'll be interested and stimulated enough to want to get to work on this swimming and water-safety, either directly for your own benefit; or to help someone else. Just who that is will depend on whether you're a parent or teacher—or both, basically.

Even so, this isn't exclusively an instructional guide for children, although we did start off with the baby. Well, most of us do.

I'd hate to think that lots of grown-ups in need of help in the water automatically rejected this particular book because they were put-off by the sections for infants and schools. I shouldn't think a parent would be, would you?

Anyway, it's for you if you need help with your early swimming efforts. I hope you will. Keep in touch.

H.R.

Index

Index